SOCIAL PSYCHOLOGY

JOHN W. KINCH
PROFESSOR OF SOCIOLOGY
CALIFORNIA STATE UNIVERSITY, SAN FRANCISCO

McGRAW-HILL BOOK COMPANY

NEW YORK   ST. LOUIS   SAN FRANCISCO   DÜSSELDORF   JOHANNESBURG
KUALA LUMPUR   LONDON   MEXICO   MONTREAL   NEW DELHI
PANAMA   RIO DE JANEIRO   SINGAPORE   SYDNEY   TORONTO

PHOTO CREDITS

CHAPTERS ONE, FOUR, SIX, SEVEN   Susan Ylvisaker, Jeroboam
CHAPTER TWO   Sam Coombs, Photofind
CHAPTERS THREE, NINE, TEN, ELEVEN   Roger Lubin, Jeroboam
CHAPTERS FIVE, EIGHT   David Powers, Jeroboam

This book was set in Janson by American
Book–Stratford Press, Inc. The editors were
David Edwards, Phyllis T. Dulan, and
Judith Chaffin; the designer was Janet
Durey Bollow; and the production super-
visor was Joan M. Oppenheimer. The draw-
ings were done by John Foster.
The printer and binder was The Murray
Printing Company.

SOCIAL PSYCHOLOGY

LIBRARY OF CONGRESS CATALOGING IN PUBLICATION DATA

Kinch, John W.
  Social psychology.
  1. Social psychology. I. Title.
[DNLM: 1. Psychology, Social. HM 251 K51s 1973]
HM251.K514   301.1   72–11722
ISBN 0–07–034569–4
ISBN 0–07–034570–8 (pbk)

234567890 MUMU 7987654

TO MY WIFE, HONOR

CONTENTS

PREFACE

This book is an attempt to fill a need in the teaching of social psychology. It is designed to provide the student with a brief, concise statement of the general principles and concepts of social psychology. In it he will find the core of the field. From it he should be able to move out into specialized areas that interest him.

In several years of teaching courses in social psychology, I found that the standard-length texts were not satisfactory. In their attempt to cover all the research and theory of the vast area of social psychology they tend to cloud the concepts with details and lose any overall continuity. The present text attempts to provide the core or outline for the course; the instructor should assign supplementary material that will provide more information about areas of interest to his students. The list of suggested references at the end of each chapter should be helpful; those marked with an asterisk (*) are available in paperback form. The instructor can use this text plus several supplementary readings without overburdening the student with either excessive reading material or high cost. A number of excellent books of readings are available in paperback editions.

The text does not assume that the student has had a course in either sociology or psychology, although an introductory course in either of these areas would be to his advantage. The aim of the text is to give the student an understanding of the perspective of social psychology as a scientific discipline with the goal of understanding human social behavior. It is not an attempt to popularize the field, nor does it provide social psychological knowledge aimed at solving social problems or improving personal adjustment. However, the author feels strongly that the concepts and principles learned from reading this book should have concrete referents for the student in his everyday life. The text is written with the aim of getting him to relate the material presented to the world he lives in.

To this end, I have found it valuable with my own students to assign a novel or a play along with the text and other supplementary material. If the student can identify the social psychological principles and concepts demonstrated in a novel like Claude Brown's *Manchild in the Promised Land* or in a play like Jean Genet's *The Balcony*, then he can be reasonably confident that he has mastered those principles and concepts.

Unfortunately, it is impossible to acknowledge all those who have contributed to this book. Over the years, the relative contributions of professors, students, colleagues, and friends get mixed with the contributions from texts, readings, and research so that the author is never completely certain where his ideas come from. The texts of Alfred R. Lindesmith and Anselm L. Strauss and Tamotsu Shibutani have been particularly influential in my thinking. My colleague Professor Fred Thalhiemer has helped immeasurably with his encouragement and criticism. Some of my colleagues will undoubtedly find their ideas sprinkled throughout the book. To all those who have provided ideas and stimulation for this book, I acknowledge my thanks and indebtedness.

JOHN W. KINCH

ONE

INTRODUCTION

As human beings our very existence depends on our relationships with others. To explain an individual's behavior, his personality, the way he thinks, or the way he feels requires that we think of him in a social context. He is seldom free from the influence of his associates. Their existence, either imagined or real, is constantly directing the way he thinks, feels, and acts. Life moves from one social exchange to another so that even when one is alone he is reviewing past exchanges and contemplating those to come.

You and I are engaged in a form of social interaction: I as the author of this text and you as the reader. I have initiated the action by writing these words; you have reacted by reading them. In this seemingly simple exchange, we have demonstrated our essentially human nature, differentiating ourselves from all nonhuman animals. We have communicated by use of high-order abstractions and have symbolically conceived of ourselves as objects in a social environment.

The social psychologist recognizes men's social nature and attempts to account for the behavior and psychological processes of individuals in terms of the positions they occupy in social structures, organizations, and groups. Social psychology develops models or theories to explain men's behavior, exposes these models to real-world experiences, and, finally, accepts or rejects them in terms of how well they account for the experiences observed.

Actually, every person operates in his everyday life with some model that allows him to interpret his own experiences and to anticipate how others will react to him. The social psychologist is required to use systematic and coherent theoretical structures for his conceptual schemes and to make observations that will serve as bases for confident generalizations.

SOCIAL PSYCHOLOGY AS A SCIENTIFIC DISCIPLINE

The term "social psychology" implies both a *method of study* and a *substantive area of interest*. Most social psychologists conceive of themselves as scholars engaged in *scientific* investigations of the substantive area that we call social psychology. Since there are no sharp boundaries delimiting the content of the discipline, it seems appropriate to first briefly consider the method of science to be employed before attempting a definition of the area.

Few terms in the English language have been misunderstood more than the word "science." The confusion about the meaning of "science" cannot be cleared up in this text; however, it is important that we clarify our thinking on the topic before we go further in the discussion of social psychology.

Science can be conceived as the interplay of *observations and ideas*. Although this statement is not satisfactory in itself, it seems an excellent start for clarifying misunderstanding. Incidental *observations* on the part of the scientist bring forth *ideas* that seem to account for what was noticed. These ideas in turn direct the scientist to new and more systematic observations. The new observations require rejection, revision, or reinforcement of the idea that originated them. Through this process, the ideas become more elaborate and the observations become more systematic. For the word "ideas," we substitute the word "theory"; and the observations become the research methods and their resulting data that we use in verifying these new theories.

We can say that science is the process whereby verifiable statements about causal relationships (ideas or explanations) are originated and empirically tested. Through this process, a scientific discipline emerges. The discipline defines the subject matter to be covered and thus the nature of the data appropriate for testing, but the process is essentially the same regardless of the discipline.

A *theory* may be thought of as a set of interrelated propositions about some area of concern. A theory in social psychology, then, is a set of statements that systematically attempt to explain the behavior of the individual in terms of his involvement in the social structure. These are the *ideas* of social psychology. From these theories, certain propositions, or hypotheses, are selected to be tested. The hypotheses are tested by systematic observations of the behavior (or other phenomenon) to which the statement refers. The methods used for the collection of social psychological evidence are considered in some detail in the next chapter.

In practice, the social psychologist does not always work as systematically as the above discussion might imply. He frequently expands ideas into great detail without supporting evidence. At times, he is guilty of giving the impression that the generalizations he presents have been generated under carefully controlled conditions, when in fact they are only hunches that occurred to him as he watched his own children.

The goal of social psychology is the development of a body of knowledge regarding the nature of man as a social being. As in any science, this endeavor takes the form of a systematic collection of verified generalizations and explanations.

THE SUBJECT MATTER OF SOCIAL PSYCHOLOGY

We find some disagreement on the question of the content or substance of social psychology. Occasional sharp differences arise about what constitutes the legitimate concern of the discipline. The boundaries that demarcate social psychology from other social sciences are in no way established. With this in mind, it seems wise to begin our discussion of the substance of social psychology by considering those general points upon which we might expect some consensus.

The following statement from Gordon Allport's[1] study of the historical background of modern social psychology is a useful starting point:

> With few exceptions, social psychologists regard their discipline as *an attempt to understand how the thought, feeling, and behavior of individuals are influenced by the actual, imagined, or implied presence of other human beings.* The term "implied presence" refers to the many activities the individual carries out because of his position (role) in a complex social structure and his membership in a cultural group.

Definitions or statements regarding social psychology given in some of the major textbooks in the discipline show some general agreement as to what is the appropriate area of study.

Krech, Crutchfield, and Ballachey[2] state: "Social psychology may therefore be broadly viewed as the science of the behavior of the individual in society." For Sherif and Sherif[3] it is "the scientific study of the experience and behavior of individuals in relation to social stimulus situations." Hartley

[1] Gordon Allport, "The Historical Background of Modern Social Psychology," in Gardner Lindzey and Elliot Aronson (eds.), *The Handbook of Social Psychology*, 2d ed., Addison-Wesley Publishing Co. Inc., Reading, Mass., 1968, vol. I, p. 3.
[2] David Krech, Richard S. Crutchfield, and Egerton L. Ballachey, *Individual in Society*, McGraw-Hill Book Company, New York, 1962, p. 4.
[3] Muzafer Sherif and Carolyn W. Sherif, *An Outline of Social Psychology*, rev. ed., Harper & Row, Publishers, New York, 1969, p. 8.

and Hartley[4] indicate that social psychology "is primarily focused upon those aspects of social behavior found when man interacts with another in manifest social relationships"; whereas Lindesmith and Strauss[5] are concerned with "explaining behavior of individuals as it is controlled, influenced or limited by the social environment." Most seem to agree with Shibutani[6] when he points out that "social psychologists are not concerned with all of the things that men do; their attention is focused only upon those regularities in human behavior that arise out of the fact that men are participants in social groups."

We may consider these statements as reflective of the general area of agreement within social psychology. Let us turn now to some of the variations.

VARIATIONS IN SOCIAL PSYCHOLOGY

The variety of approaches to social psychology can be accounted for, in part, by the various disciplines within which the individual who calls himself a social psychologist has been trained. Sociology, psychology, and anthropology all have contributed to the area that we call social psychology, and all have brought to it differing orientations. Courses in social psychology are taught in all three of these departments in many universities and colleges. The orientation of these courses differs markedly from one department to the next; yet there is overlap, and increasingly those oriented in one discipline are using within their courses the research and writings of persons from other disciplines.

In anthropology, very little attention was given to the individual, his personality, and his makeup until about 1930.

[4] Eugene L. Hartley and Ruth E. Hartley, *Fundamentals of Social Psychology*, Alfred A. Knopf, Inc., New York, 1952, p. 5.
[5] Alfred R. Lindesmith and Anselm L. Strauss, *Social Psychology*, 3d ed., Holt, Rinehart & Winston, Inc., New York, 1968, p. 3.
[6] Tamotsu Shibutani, *Society and Personality*, Prentice-Hall, Inc., Englewood Cliffs, N.J., 1961, p. 20.

Rather, generalizations concerning primitive and preliterate societies, common in early anthropology, focused on the discovery of cultural factors common to all societies. In an intellectual movement that began in the 1930s, anthropology was conceived as the study of culture and personality. This approach of such anthropologists as Edward Sapir, Ralph Linton, and Ruth Benedict has been popularized particularly by Margaret Mead and has been absorbed into the mainstream of anthropology. The anthropologist's concern with culture and cultural differences has had a profound effect on current social psychology. Materials gathered by ethnologists have frequently contradicted findings of those sociologists and psychologists who had based their conclusions on evidence gathered from a single society. The anthropologist, particularly by his emphasis on culture and cultural differences, has attempted to arrive at a body of knowledge that accounts for the nature of man. He has created and applied social psychological principles in an attempt to accomplish this end.

In psychology, the situation was considerably different. Toward the end of the nineteenth century, social psychological notions were beginning to influence the thinking of psychologists. In 1908, William McDougall's influential book *Social Psychology* was published. Until quite recently, however, social psychology was seen as a specialty within psychology, rather than as an integral part of the discipline. It did move from the position of a minor field within the larger discipline to a subdivision with considerable stature. The varieties of social psychology within psychology today make difficult any definitive statement regarding its significance in that discipline. Freudian psychoanalytical theory, Lewin's field theory, and contemporary social learning theory are all at least in part social psychological and all are considered part of the discipline of psychology, yet they differ as much from each other in orientation and method as they differ from approaches in anthropology and sociology. Those persons in psychology departments who have called themselves social psychologists have gained a respected position in the discipline. Their research has directed the attention and appreciation of those in other specialties to the roles of the group, the social structure, and the society in the operation of psychological processes.

In many ways, the development of social psychology within sociology was similar to its development and influence within psychology; however, there was one major difference. Social psychology was never thought of as a minor specialty within the general body of social theory that the sociologist dealt with. From the earliest developments in sociology, social psychological principles were given central recognition. Most of the influential sociologists, both past and present, have dealt with social psychological problems as if they were integral and central features of sociological concern.

Such early sociologists as Emile Durkheim, Georg Simmel, W. I. Thomas, Max Weber, and Gabriel Tarde studied groups as interacting human beings and could hardly avoid concern with the individuals whose participation in the group made up the patterns of interaction they were studying. Sociology in the United States has been profoundly influenced by pragmatists such as John Dewey and George Herbert Mead, whose social philosophy was directed at new ways of looking at man and society. These philosophers advocated a change in the ways of looking at man and society—from the study of stable forms of composition and structure to the dynamic concern with activity and change. Rather than description of things in terms of the structure of the person or social institution, they encouraged the study of *how things worked*, both in terms of the individual organism and the group or institution. Mead believed that the very nature of man—the characteristics that distinguished him from lower animals—emerged out of his adaption to the exigencies of living in groups.

With this intellectual climate as a background, it is little wonder that social psychology has been central to most sociology.

This is not to contend that all sociologists are really social psychologists. On the contrary, some are quite convinced that social phenomena can be and should be investigated without explicit attention being paid to individual persons. Industrial organizations, political institutions, and the mass media are examples of these phenomena.

We have tried to show in this introduction that in some respects there are many social psychologies. Few, if any, social psychologists look for the day when all will converge into one grand social psychology that all can agree upon. For the most part, social psychology has gained its stature because of the increasing recognition by those in different fields that their specialties could not satisfactorily explain all that seemed relevant to their concern. The psychologist found that he could not always account for the behavior he was observing, and the sociologist found it hard to show how institutions changed. Slowly they came to the realization that men never live completely independent of groups, and almost anything that man does is in one way or another effected by his association with others. Still, when the psychologist uses social psychological principles or findings to account for uniformities in individual behavior he may be using quite a different social psychology than the sociologist who uses social psychological findings to account for the manner in which political institutions change. We see little reason to hope for or to desire complete convergence.

We have spent these first pages on the diversity of social psychology for two reasons. First, the student of social psychology should be aware that there are these differing ways of approaching the field, even though they cannot all be satisfactorily covered in this text. Second, the reader should realize that this short book presents a particular social psychology, rather than all of social psychology.

THE INTERACTIONIST APPROACH

The particular social psychology of this text has traditionally found its greatest support among sociologists. The intellectual traditions that provide the most profound source of ideas for this approach can be found in the writings of sociologists like Charles H. Cooley and W. I. Thomas and of the American pragmatic philosophers, notably John Dewey and George Herbert Mead. This orientation in social psychology is usually labeled the *interactionist* approach. Again, *it is but one of many possible ways* of looking at the things men do. The interactionist approach is characterized by the central contention that the interactions of men produce both human nature and the social order. Three propositions are basic to this approach:

1. The individual's personality—the distinctive patterns of behavior that characterize him as an individual—results from and is reinforced by his day-to-day association with those about him.
2. The individual's behavior or conduct follows a direction that is the result of reciprocal give-and-take of interdependent men who are adjusting to one another.
3. The culture of the group is a reflection of those agreements about proper conduct that emerge and are reinforced by man's continual communication as people collectively come to terms with life's conditions.

Social interaction, then, is seen as the source of the individual's personality, and the guide and motive for his behavior. From social interaction evolve the structure of the group and eventually the institutions that make up society. These transactions can be accomplished only by those facilities that are uniquely characteristic of human beings: *the abilities to think abstractly, to form perceptual objects of themselves, and to engage in purposive and moral conduct.* The interactionist believes that these distinctively human characteristics enable man to rise above other animals and that the social psychologist should give his attention to these characteristics as he attempts to unravel the mystery of human existence.

TWO

SOURCES OF EVIDENCE

The nature of evidence is not an easy topic to deal with realistically in social psychology. The topic is based on the question: How do we know? Traditionally, this question has been answered within the discipline by statements to the effect that we utilize the scientific method and apply the tools of the discipline such as experimentation, surveys, observational techniques, and the like. This is all very true, but it tends to give a false picture of where we are in social psychology today. If we were allowed to use only those generalizations that have been verified by the application of the most rigorous research methodology, the content of this book would be short indeed!

This chapter is deliberately entitled "sources of evidence" rather than "methods of research" or some other title frequently used in social psychology, in order to emphasize the general questions: How do we know what we claim we know? There was a hint of this in the first chapter. How does any individual know what he knows? The social psychologist uses essentially the same model used by each of us in our everyday life; however, as he moves along, he imposes on himself certain rules that he feels will be advantageous in helping him reach his goal. First, we must look at his goals, and then we can consider the regulations that govern his endeavor.

GOALS OF SOCIAL PSYCHOLOGY

The goals of social psychology are to *discover* and *explain* the relationships between society and the individual; included here are relationships between individuals, between individuals and groups, between groups, and between groups and society. We cannot understand these goals without asking what "explanation" means in this context. Some have said the goals of social psychology are to predict, to understand, and to explain. Stating the goals in this manner should help to create a clearer understanding of the processes employed by the scientist. We explain through making generalized statements about relationships found to exist between the phenomena under investigation. These statements are not merely descriptive of the actual observations made, but they also are descriptive of the general class of objects under investigation. For example, a study by sociologist James Coleman[1] revealed that children from lower-class homes showed a considerable variation in their intellectual achievement. Some did well in school, some did poorly. This was a discovery from a carefully conceived and executed research project. However, this discovery of what is, is not in itself an explanation. The social psychologist wants to know why. What accounts for the difference? What "caused" some children to do well while others failed? In this study, the investigators looked at several factors—the varying per pupil expenditures of the different schools, size of the classes, the presence or absence of ability groupings (reading groups), and the like. One factor seemed to make a significant difference: the pattern of characteristics of the other children in the same

[1] James S. Coleman, *et al.*, *Equality of Educational Opportunity*, U.S. Government Printing Office, 1966.

class. If the lower-class children had classmates who came from advantaged homes, they did well; however, if they were in classes where all the other children were from similarly deprived homes, they did poorly.

Now we are beginning to explain. We have discovered that there is a relationship between the characteristics of the peers in the child's class and his achievement. We assume that this is in some way a causal relationship. Since logic rules out the possibility that the children's lack of intellectual achievement leads to (causes) the socioeconomic characteristics of children in their class, it seems reasonable to believe that the distribution of these characteristics contributes to intellectual achievement.

It is important to note that this is not simply a description of the 600,000 children whom Coleman studied, but that his findings can be generalized and put in the form of a prediction. That is, we would predict that, if we were to take a group of children from lower-class homes and place them in schools with children from advantaged homes, they would do better than a similar group of children placed in a school attended exclusively by lower-class children.

In our example, we have clearly reached the stage where predictions can be made with some confidence. But have we arrived at understanding? We would probably want to go further and ask such questions as: What is it about the interaction and association with peers from advantaged homes that makes the poor children do better? What is it specifically about living in an advantaged home that affects school performance? The more we fill in the gaps in our knowledge the more we can say we understand. Prediction and understanding are the essence of explanation—that is, the goal of science.

THE RESTRICTIONS OF EMPIRICAL SCIENCE

If the goal of the social psychologist is to discover and explain certain relationships, just how does he go about this discovery? We might start by saying that like any discoverer he goes out and looks. The analogy with the geographical explorer is instructive. When the explorer first sets out he has very little to go on. He has heard speculation as to what he will find, but no one knows for sure. So it is with the social psychologist who moves into a new field. He has some hunches and some intuitive understanding, but mostly he is just looking. As the explorer makes discoveries he records them. His fellow discoverer who comes that way will use his records as guides and will add to them new discoveries until eventually a precise map of the area has been devised. So, we could say that the social psychologist is developing maps of generalizations that explain his area of concern. We call the maps theories. The specific statements in the theory that tell the investigator what he is likely to find are called hypotheses. It is important to remember that all scientific explanation ends with theories. Here the analogy with the map is particularly useful. When the explorer starts out, he makes up a map primarily on the basis of hunches and speculation. He may know from an earlier expedition that there are islands 100 miles to the east and that the current runs due north along the coast. The natives claim that sailors once came with furs from the northeast. On the basis of these bits and pieces, along with his knowledge of the sea, he theorizes about the nature of the area and hypothesizes that he will find land if he heads in a southeasterly direction. He draws a rough map of his speculation. As he sails the area and makes more and more discoveries, he puts them on his map. Each addition means that there are fewer places on the map left to speculation. So it is with theory. In the initial development of a theory, the social psychologist must rely heavily upon intuition, speculation, and incidental observations he has casually made. But as his observations increase and become more systematic, his map becomes more precise. His theory is more rigorous and less reliant on guesses and speculation.

It should be clear, then, that when the social psychologist

goes out to look he does not move randomly or without fore-thought. He takes with him a set of hypotheses and these hypotheses profoundly influence what he discovers. Observations do not speak for themselves. To be meaningfully under-stood, they must fit together into some type of framework. This is the theory.

This is not different from discovery in everyday life. If you get up in the morning and find that your car will not start, the first thing you do is to think of a hypothesis to account for why it will not start. You consider the hypothesis that the battery is dead. Then you seek evidence that will confirm or disprove your hypothesis. You turn on the light switch. If the lights go on with full strength, you must reject your hypothe-sis and consider something else. If they do not go on, you have discovered evidence that supports your hypothesis. As in scientific research, supporting a hypothesis is not proving it. Your battery may still be perfect, but the cable may be loose.

There is a difference between your discovery and that of the social psychologist. The social psychologist's theories and hypotheses must be of a general nature so that meaningful generalizations may be made.

Let us see what rules we have imposed on the social psy-chologist as he works toward the goals of his science. First, we require that he start out with a set of hypotheses. They may be vague and hazy or they may be formal and precise, but he must have something to guide him in the observations he will make. Second, even though we allow him to start with hunches and intuition, we require that all his observations, which revise and firm up his theory, must be *empirical* in nature. By "empirical" we mean that the observation must be of the "real world." That is, we require that his generalization be verifiable by other competent scientists observing the same world. Like the explorer whose map is worthless unless it can be related to some part of the world, the scientist's theory is worthless unless its concepts refer to the empirical world.

Third, we require that he accept as his guiding principle the goals of social psychology. By this we mean that he must be committed to discovering and explaining some aspect of the relationship between man and society. He may have other motives as well—to improve the world, to get his candidate elected, or whatever—but to be a social psychologist, he must agree that discovery and explanation are his primary goals. This is important because once he has accepted this principle, his research will be governed by a number of other regulations that follow logically.

For example, if he is to reach his goals he must be *honest*, both with himself and others. He must report his results as he finds them, not as he hopes they would have come out. He must utilize every device necessary to insure that his own biases are not interfering with the outcome of his observation. He must agree to report findings whether they support his hypothesis or refute it, because his ultimate aim is not to *prove* his hypothesis but to *test* it. So, when we suggest that the scientist should be *systematic* and *objective*, what we are saying is that his scientific behavior should reduce the likelihood that biases and extraneous factors will interfere with the outcome and that his discoveries and explanation will be an accurate reflection of the world that he studies.

We might put it another way and say the social psychologist is concerned with discovering the *truth* about human social relationships. However, we should be certain that we agree about and understand the use of the word "truth" in this context. When we speak of "scientific truth," we mean that statements or generalizations will hold up under repeated observations by qualified observers.

RESEARCH TECHNIQUES
Regardless of the specific research techniques that the social psychologist chooses to utilize in his investigation of his subject matter, he always in one way or the other is applying the general method, common to all science—that is, ideas leading

to observations, leading to new ideas, and so forth. As we discuss those techniques most generally used by the social psychologist, keep in mind the overall goal of the development of generalizations designed to explain the relationships that exist between the individual and society.

Incidental Observations

In the early stages of development of ideas and theories in social psychology, rather unsystematic observations of the behavior of persons are likely to be used. The social psychologist may start to formulate his ideas from reading the findings of others' research or discussing ideas with his colleagues. He may test out an idea about how people relate to each other by watching his children; but the social psychologist is not ready to make a generalization based on this alone. First, he must subject his ideas to the test of more observations. His second step may again be to make incidental observations, but now with a little more care since he knows what he is looking for. For example, he may notice that his two-year-old, when placed in a playpen with another child his age, plays by himself and recognizes the other's existence only when he comes into direct contact with him. He muses, "Cooperative play I have noted in my five-year-old must take a more highly developed understanding of the world than could be expected in two-year-olds." So he becomes curious (a virtue held by all good scientists). The next day he stops by the library to see if something has already been written on the subject. Not satisfied with what he can find from others' work, he stops by the day-care center where children from two to five years of age are kept while their parents are at work. Here he has even more material for observations. He looks around to see which children are playing with others and which are playing by themselves. He notes that with a few exceptions the younger children are much more self-centered than the older children. This simple example is not atypical of the way many of our ideas get started. Ideally these ideas, as they are confirmed by incidental observations, lead the social psychologist to even more systematic observations so that he can be confident that his own biases or expectations have not blinded him and influenced his observations.

In doing observation studies, the researcher must always consider the effects of his observing on the thing under observation. If you were interested in knowing what proportion of automobile drivers ordinarily come to a complete stop at a stop sign, you would not stand in plain sight next to the sign with your clipboard and pencil. A driver might well be influenced to make a complete stop when he sees you there for fear that you are taking down license numbers. The observer's presence is affecting what is being observed. We can take care of this problem in two ways: by getting closer to the object under observation or by getting farther away from it.

Adherents of the school of thought in sociology known as ethnomethodology contend that the only way to understand persons is to become intimately involved with them in their groups and take on their perspective as the perspective for analysis. This extreme form of what has been called "participant observation" has proved very useful in some areas of study. By becoming a member of the group, joining in their activities, and sharing their perspective, the investigator himself can minimize his effect on the ongoing activity and yet is in an ideal position to observe this activity. Because he is not seen as an outsider coming in to investigate, the group members have no reason to change their behavior patterns.

Systematic Observations

The division between incidental and systematic observations is certainly one of degree. As observations become more systematic, several factors are added. In the unsystematic observations of the incidental observer, hypotheses are likely to be only vaguely formulated. They are hunches, sometimes never made explicit even in the mind of the observer. As his ideas firm up into the form of theories, his hypotheses are more explicit, and his observations begin to become more systematic. In the example used above, the social psychologist who has the ideas about children's sociability might continue his investigation by stating a hypothesis that children between the ages of two and five years will show an increasing interest in and ability to play cooperatively with other children their own age. On the basis of this hypothesis, he might train some of the students in his social psychology class, who will go to all the nursery schools in the city where they will sit and watch the children play over a period of several days. They will systematically record the number of minutes each child spends interacting with other children, classify this interaction (say, into cooperation or competition), and finally bring all the data together for a statistical analysis to see just what differences exist. The students, if well trained, would stay out of sight of the children (ideally behind a one-way screen) so that their observations would not bother the children in their play. In addition, the attendants in the schools would not be informed of the intention of the study so that their interaction with the children would not inadvertently interfere with the outcome of the investigation.

Experimentation

In all of the observation techniques discussed so far, the researcher exerted no control over his subject matter. He simply observed the persons as they behave in their everyday life. When the investigator begins to deliberately introduce factors into the situation or to control the behavior of his subjects, we have the beginnings of an experiment. If the social psychologist of our example deliberately took his two-year-old and sat him next to the neighbor's two-year-old to see how they react, we would say that he was experimenting. Some ethnomethodologists deliberately "disturb the scene," as they say, in order to observe reactions. Garfinkel[2] tells of an experi-

---

[2] This is by no means a complete description of ethnomethodology, which has many other facets that cannot be discussed here. For a fuller

ment in which his investigators deliberately withheld their responses in ordinary social intercourse to see how people would react to such behavior. These simple experiments are similar to the incidental observations we discussed earlier. Usually, when the word "experimentation" is used in social psychology, we think of more controlled settings in which the investigator manipulates the subjects and the situation so that he can become relatively certain of the variables accounting for the observations he makes.

There are many types of experimental designs, each with drawbacks, each with special application. The classical design calls for the comparison of two groups that are matched or otherwise selected so that they are as similar as possible. Then, to one group, called the experimental group, the investigator introduces what is called a stimulus, or treatment variable. The other group, the control group, remains exactly the same as the experimental group but is not subjected to the treatment variable. Finally, the two groups are measured on an effect variable to see what resulted from the introduction of the stimulus. An example will help to clarify this method. Suppose we wished to test the hypothesis that the assignment of a book of readings helps students to learn social psychology. We might start out with a large number of students (say 100), test them on a number of variables that we feel might affect their learning of the course, and on the basis of these tests divide them into two *equal* groups. We would be sure that each group has the same distribution of students in terms of IQ, previous knowledge of social psychology, grades in college, and the like. To one group, the experimental group, we would introduce the book of readings (the treatment variable). The control group would not have this assignment but would otherwise have the same learning experience—the same instructor, the same text, the same lectures, and so forth. We

---

examination see Harold Garfinkel, *Studies in Ethnomethodology,* Prentice-Hall, Inc., Englewood Cliffs, N.J., 1967.

would use the final examination as the effect variable. Since the two groups would be identical in all respects except for the assignment of the book of readings, we can be relatively certain that any difference on the final examination must be due to (or caused by) the additional assignment.

The perceptive student might well find faults in the design as described. How can we be certain that the two groups are identical? How do we know that the final examination really measured what the student learned in social psychology? Many critical questions can be asked about a simple design such as this. If the questions can be answered with some degree of satisfaction and if the differences in outcome between the experimental group and the control group are larger than could be expected by chance, then we can feel with confidence that our evidence supports our hypothesis. The student should note the control that was needed in order for the experimenter to carry out the experiment. We must be able to administer tests to students, to assign them to different experimental and control groups, to require that the experimental group be assigned the book, and so on.

The experiment has some valuable advantages over other methods. It goes a long way toward reducing the possibility of the intrusion of personal bias and other extraneous variables and is, therefore, one of the most objective methods used in social psychology. It is the only method in which it is possible to study the effects of one variable at a time, holding constant the effects of other factors. Probably its biggest drawbacks are its need for manipulative control, which cannot always be obtained, and the unexplained effects of these manipulations on the outcome of the experiment.

As we have implied earlier, experiments take many forms. We should not leave our discussion without mentioning the distinction often made between the laboratory experiment and the natural or field experiment. The laboratory experiment is the most controlled method employed in modern-day social psychology. The technique became popular when social psychologists discovered that they could study small groups in much the same way as the physical world is studied by physicists, that is, by bringing the subject into a "laboratory" and, under carefully controlled conditions, simulating certain features of the natural environment. The method has proved extremely valuable, especially in areas that are impossible to study under "natural" conditions.

The natural experiment varies only in degree from the laboratory experiment. The introduction of a book of readings into a social psychology course is an example of the natural experiment, in that the subjects were not placed in an artificial setting, but rather were asked to do about what they would expect to do when they signed up for the class. This might be contrasted with a laboratory experiment such as that done by Solomon Asch,[3] in which subjects were placed in a room and asked to judge which of three lines on a screen before them was the closest in length to a fourth line nearby. This experiment presents a much more artificial setting than the field experiment. The question is frequently raised: Is it legitimate to generalize from what is discovered in the laboratory to the natural world outside the lab? The answer is too complicated for consideration in a text of this size; however, we can say that carefully considered generalizations based on laboratory studies appear to be just as valid as those derived from natural, but less controlled, experiments. As with all the methods under consideration, the validity of the experimental method depends to a great extent on the care and skill of the investigator who applies the method and on the understanding and sophistication used in interpreting the results.

Introspection

It is not always possible for the investigator to observe behavior pertinent to the hypotheses that he is studying, and

[3] Solomon Asch, "Opinion and Social Pressure," *Scientific American*, vol. 193, no. 5, pp. 31–35, November 1955.

there are times when his subject matter has to do with feeling and attitudes that cannot readily be observed. In the study of prejudice it may be possible to observe a person acting in a discriminatory way toward members of a minority group; however, we are not certain whether this reaction results from a personal prejudice or from some other factor (he may be carrying out company policy). Another person who shows no outward discrimination may be deeply prejudiced; but, because of the situation (say that he is running for political office), his behavior is not consistent with his attitude. If we cannot observe him over a long period of time and in a variety of settings, the only way available to determine his attitude is to ask him to report his own feelings.

This usually takes the form of an interview, a questionnaire, a rating scale, or an opinion poll. Each of these methods has been used with considerable success in social psychological research. Some of the disadvantages are obvious. When you ask a person what he has done, how he feels, or what his attitude is you get reliable answers only if he can and does tell the truth. The data obtained may also be inaccurate because the questions are poorly conceived and presented, or because the respondent is careless or ignorant, or because he has reason to conceal the truth. Although subtle devices have been developed to get respondents to feel they can give open, truthful answers, in some areas of investigation, self-reporting of any kind yields doubtful results. Areas about which the respondent feels highly sensitive or under pressures to give socially desirable responses must be handled with extreme care.

The Questionnaire
Of the various techniques considered, the questionnaire is probably most often used. It has the great advantage of allowing for the analysis of many variables using a sizable sample. Space does not permit a detailed description of this method, but the student should become aware of types of analyses made possible by this method as compared with the experi-

ment or observation methods already discussed. From the
questionnaire, it is possible to obtain information on the characteristics of the respondent, such as his age, sex, schooling,
economic background, and the like, as well as information
about his actions (for example, how he voted) and the way he
feels. In the experiment, the interest is usually focused on a
particular group or setting; in the questionnaire, the concern is
with the interrelationships of respondents' attributes and feelings or attitudes. For example, in a questionnaire study of
college students, it would be possible to test the hypothesis
that the further one goes in college the more liberal his
political attitudes become. On a questionnaire sent to a sample
of college students, we could ask each respondent how many
years he had attended college, then ask a series of questions
about his political attitude. By using these last questions as a
scale for measuring liberal versus conservative attitudes, we
could assign each respondent a score on political attitudes. By
correlating his scale score with his year in college, we could
test our hypothesis. This method frequently employs statistical
analysis, both in development of attitude scales and in the
correlational analyses to test the hypotheses. Note that the
individuals are not studied as members of groups; rather, the
analyses deal with the understanding of the relationships between the attributes of the individual respondent (his year in
school) and his feeling (political attitude). Note also that the
same study could have correlated political attitude with age,
sex, economic background, or any other background variable
that was included on the questionnaire. If we had asked questions about the individual's voting behavior (how he voted in
the last election), we could correlate these background variables with political behavior as well as attitudes. The questionnaire method in one form or another has been used in almost
every area of social psychology, from questioning persons who
were involved in riots to studying attitudes toward new teaching methods in the public schools.

The Interview

The questionnaire generally is a structured set of questions that the individual reads and responds to by himself. In contrast, the interview is a technique in which the investigator, or his representative (the interviewer), asks the questions of the respondent. One advantage of the questionnaire is that it can be administered to a large number of persons at one time; on the other hand, the interview has the advantage of being considerably more flexible. The interviewer, if well trained and skillful, can determine if the respondent understands the question the way it was intended and thus can strive for a more reliable response.

The interview, when used in a highly structured form in which the questions are read verbatim to each respondent, differs from the questionnaire only slightly. However, in some interview settings the interviewer is given considerably more latitude in eliciting responses. In using a conversational form, a great deal of flexibility is provided for spontaneous probing of attitudes held by the respondent. To use this technique effectively, the interviewer must be particularly skillful and must be well aware of the purpose of the investigation. A further advantage of the interview is that the skilled interviewer can record the behavior of the respondent as he reacts to the questions being asked.

Projective Methods

Even with anonymous questionnaires and skillful interviewers, many social psychologists have remained skeptical of the method of direct questioning in obtaining responses in areas of sensitivity for the respondent. When the individual knows that society would not condone his hostile feeling or his antisocial behavior, he may not be able to clearly admit his feeling even to himself—let alone reveal them to an investigator. In response to this problem, psychologists have developed a series of methods called projective techniques. In some ways, this technique is an extension of the interview; it employs a psychological mechanism called projection in which the respondent "projects" into his responses his underlying attitudes or perceptions. The approach usually takes the form of requiring the subject to give his impressions of relatively ambiguous and standardized material. When he tells a story about a picture or describes what he sees in an ink-blot design, he reveals his inner feelings. In telling his story, he is revealing things about himself that he would not have told had he been questioned directly. For example, if the subject describes a man who is feeling very sad because he has hurt someone he really loves, the investigator is alerted to the possibility that the subject is actually telling things about his own inner feeling that he might not reveal directly. This technique has been used most effectively with children, whose linguistic skills limit their responses to direct questions, and with mentally disturbed persons whose gross personality disorders are easily identified. In more conventional social psychological research, the method is limited in the types of information obtainable. For this reason, it is not widely used outside of clinical psychology.

Content Analysis

In all the techniques described up to this point, the investigator must have some type of direct contact with the individual or group being studied, either by direct observation or through questioning. Although these are by far the most frequently used techniques, there are others that do not require such direct contact. One such method is content analysis, which includes a variety of procedures but usually takes the form of coding and categorization of written or spoken material so that a quantitative analysis can be made. For example, we might have the hypothesis that as an election campaign draws closer to election day, the candidates discuss the characters and personalities of their opponents more and the issues less. We could collect the texts of the speeches made by the candidates and the advertisements placed in the newspapers and run on television at various times during the campaign. Then, by carefully coding the content of the speeches and ads, we could determine how much of each was devoted to personalities and how much to issues. By comparing these proportions over time, we could test the hypothesis. Does the proportion of space or time allocated to issues decrease as the campaign comes closer to the election? This method, of course, is limited in its scope; however, when it can be applied, it has a degree of objectivity that cannot be attained by any of the other techniques.

Unobtrusive Measures

Content analysis described above has the advantage of being a nonreactive measure. That is, it does not require the investigator to have direct contact with the subject under study; therefore, his observations cannot cause a reaction that might bias the observations. The broader category of techniques that fulfill this criterion of nonreaction is called *unobtrusive measures*.[4] Examples range from comparing the racial attitudes in two colleges by rating the degree of clustering of blacks and whites in lecture halls, to counting public library withdrawals to demonstrate the effect of the introduction of television into a community.

Most of these techniques have been imitative and ingenious, but with the exception of content analysis, none have been standardized. In addition, most require that the investigator make quite a leap in his inference about the meaning of the measure. (That is, how confident can we be that seating patterns reflect racial attitudes?) However, their adherents

[4] See Eugene J. Webb, Donald T. Campbell, Richard D. Schwartz, and Lee Sechrest: *Unobtrusive Measures: Nonreactive Research in the Social Sciences*, Rand McNally & Co., Chicago, 1966.

suggest they are most valuable when used in conjunction with other techniques. Given the drawbacks inherent in most re-active techniques (questionnaires, interviews, projective tests, and so on), this approach is certainly worthy of further pursuit.

In the limited space available, we have not been able to systematically and thoroughly discuss all the advantages and disadvantages of these various techniques of social psychology. Nor have we adequately dealt with the various considerations that must go into their application. The student who would use any of these methods should do some further reading on research methods and should become familiar with the particular method before he begins. The student and the social psychologist both should always keep in mind that these techniques are only means to the end of discovery and explanation. They should keep this question always before them: Am I, through the use of this experiment, this observation, or this questionnaire, going to obtain evidence relevant to my social psychological theory?

THE SOCIOLOGY OF EVIDENCE GATHERING
IN SOCIAL PSYCHOLOGY

Too often in the discussion of research methods and their application to social psychology a very important step is left out. This is the process whereby the findings, once they have been derived from the application of these methods, become part of the content of social psychology. In other words, how does the social psychologist communicate his findings and how are these built into the coherent body of knowledge known as social psychology?

First, we have the question of communication. There are several accepted methods for communicating new findings. One widely used method is publication in one of the many professional journals that are published for this purpose. All the major sociology journals, such as the *American Sociological Review* and the *American Journal of Sociology*, publish results of social psychological research; and some journals, such as *Sociometry*, are restricted in their content to this area of research. The same is true of the psychological journals. Most social psychologists subscribe to one or more of the journals. All the major journals are available in most college libraries.

A second method for communicating social psychological findings and ideas is through papers delivered at professional meetings. Many sessions of the annual meetings of both the American Sociological Association and the American Psychological Association are devoted to papers in the area of social psychology. Here, the investigator reads the results from his study to the group of persons who have assembled to hear these reports. Although these papers do not get nearly as wide a dissemination as do published articles, they are heard by those persons who have a specialized interest in the area of investigation; and the participant is encouraged to have duplicated copies of his paper available for those who are not able to attend the session.

The third means of communication of social psychological research is through monographs or short books on various topics. These usually permit much more thorough and detailed reports of large-scale studies than are possible in the short articles published in professional journals. Some are published commercially, but most monographs are published by university presses or by the foundations that have supported the research. Some Ph.D. dissertations are turned into monographs and, thereby, the results of these studies get much wider attention.

Other means of communicating research findings are not as widely used as those mentioned above. A social psychologist may report his research as part of a larger book that he is writing on the general topic covered by his research. Or a group of researchers working on similar projects may publish a book that incorporates the findings of several research endeavors.

These various methods of communication might be called the primary sources. Others then use these sources to further put together social psychological ideas into meaningful form. Books that synthesize the findings of specific areas of social psychology may draw on all these primary sources. Textbooks in social psychology also draw on these primary sources for material for inclusion in their many sections. Books of readings are often no more than selections of research articles reprinted from journals or abstracted from monographs. In this way, the results of the research receive even wider distribution.

These sources, both primary and secondary, provide the stimuli for new ideas and the foundation for more systematic research. Observe the cycle from ideas to observations, to ideas, to observations, and so forth.

But again we must put in a word of caution. This systematic presentation of how ideas are communicated within social psychology may mislead the student into feeling that there exists a systematic procedure by which all or most of the research done in social psychology is incorporated into the larger body of knowledge that we call social psychology. No such procedure exists. Although there have been some valiant attempts to synthesize research findings in specific areas, much remains to be done and there is still confusion as to just what we know and what we do not know. For example, much research is completed but never written up and, therefore, never communicated. Other studies are written but are never accepted for publication. At each point, there are problems that make it difficult to know just where we are. Additionally, within social psychology there are many competing schools of thought; and the findings from these various approaches, although not necessarily contradictory, are not likely to be cumulative.

The message from these comments is that the student should take the material presented in this book for what it is—an attempt to fit together into a meaningful conceptual scheme what appears to be, at our present level of understanding, a coherent explanation for the relation between the individual and society. Some of the generalizations that will be presented are more firmly supported by research data than others. There is no attempt here to provide specific research support for the various statements made. Rather, it is felt that the student should consider all the material with the same skepticism. Like any true scientist, he should approach the book with a critical mind, with the faith that the material is presented with intellectual honesty, and with the conviction that, using this approach, he will arrive at new understandings both of himself as an individual and of the society in which he lives.

SUMMARY

We have covered three concerns in this chapter—research strategy, research techniques, and the actual practice of communication of research findings. The material was presented under the heading of sources of evidence in order to emphasize the goals of research—to provide evidence to evaluate social psychological theory. Although we enumerated several research techniques, it is not our intention to make researchers out of the readers. Rather we are concerned that the student of social psychology be aware of the sources of evidence and be sensitive to the problems in validating scientific statements. With this, the reader may go through the remainder of the book with a perspective that will enable him to make the most out of the material presented.

SUGGESTED REFERENCES

Denzin, Norman K.: *The Research Act,* Aldine-Atherton, Inc., Chicago, 1970.
A sophisticated analysis of the research process. Particularly valuable for the consideration of the overall design of research.

Dewey, John: *Logic: The Theory of Inquiry,* Holt, Rinehart & Winston, Inc., New York, 1938.
Classic work of the great social philosopher.

Garfinkel, Harold: *Studies in Ethnomethodology,* Prentice-Hall, Inc., Englewood Cliffs, N.J., 1967.
Considered by many to be the bible of ethnomethodology. Presents Garfinkel's approach and examples of his research.

* Holsti, Ole R.: *Content Analysis for the Social Sciences and Humanities,* Addison-Wesley Publishing Co. Inc., Reading, Mass., 1969.
A guide to content analysis.

Lindzey, Gardner, and Elliot Aronson (eds.): *The Handbook of Social Psychology,* vol. II, 2d ed., Addison-Wesley Publishing Co. Inc., Reading, Mass., 1968.
Particularly good reference articles on experimentation, attitude measurement, observation methods, interviewing, and cross-cultural research.

* Lundberg, George: *Can Science Save Us?* Longmans, Green and Company, London, 1947.
A readable description of the limitations and advantages of science as it relates to human affairs.

* Lynd, Robert S.: *Knowledge for What?* (1st ed., 1939), Grove Press, Inc., New York, 1964 (Evergreen–Black Cat Books).
A classic discussion of the social obligations of science.

* Miller, Delbert C.: *Handbook of Research Design and Social Measurement,* 2d ed., David McKay Co. Inc., New York, 1970.
An excellent catalog and description of many of the measuring instruments developed in the social sciences.

Phillips, Bernard S.: *Social Research*, The Macmillan Company, New York, 1966.
A basic text in research methodology in sociology.

* Phillips, Derek L.: *Knowledge from What?* Rand McNally & Co., Chicago, 1971.
A short, readable discussion of some of the problems involved in using the conventional research methods of the social sciences. Includes constructive suggestions to overcome difficulties.

Riley, Matilda W.: *Sociological Research: A Case Approach*, Harcourt Brace Jovanovich, Inc., New York, 1963.
Detailed discussion of a variety of well-known studies illustrating a number of approaches to data collection.

Simon, Julian L.: *Basic Research Methods in Social Science*, Random House, Inc., New York, 1969.
A detailed description of how research should be conducted. Good for the beginner who is doing his first research.

* Webb, Eugene J., Donald T. Campbell, Richard D. Schwartz, and Lee Sechrest: *Unobtrusive Measures: Nonreactive Research in the Social Sciences*, Rand McNally & Co., Chicago, 1966.
An excellent discussion of measurement in the social sciences; avoids the problems of subject reaction, which is part of much social research.

* References marked with asterisk are available in paperback.

THREE

SOCIETY
AND THE INDIVIDUAL

Understanding the relationship be-tween society and the individual is the central theme of social psychology. Various approaches to social psychology have dealt with this relationship in quite different fashions. After considering some of these variations, we will devote this chapter to an understanding of these two basic concepts, the society and the individual. This foundation will be needed for the analysis of the influences of society on the individual—the details of social psychology.

UNDERSTANDING THE RELATIONSHIP BETWEEN MAN AND SOCIETY

The various schools of thought that exist within social psychology might well be classed in terms of the way they relate man to society. The early instinct theorists placed the individual at the center of their analysis and suggested that the understanding of his inborn predis-positions to think, feel, and behave in a particular way was sufficient in explain-ing his behavior. Society was seen solely as a consequence of a large number of individuals acting out their instincts.

In contrast, the cultural determinists see society with its cultural influences as being all-pervasive. For them, the individual is born into society as no more than a flexible blob, which society molds into a human being. From this point of view, the society must be understood in order to understand the behavior of the individual.

Between these two points of view, we have what might be called the conflict explanation, which suggests that neither the individual's biological makeup nor the culture into which he is born completely explains his behavior. Rather, his manifest behavior results from a conflict between these two forces—his biological makeup and the external forces of society. Freudian psychoanalysis is an example of this point of view. On the one hand, psychoanalysis postulates an id—the innate biological impulses, instinctual in nature, that strive for fulfillment. However, these impulses are inhibited or controlled by other dimensions of the personality—the ego and the superego. The ego is seen as the storehouse of all conscious material that orients the individual to the demands of reality such as time and space. The superego is the reflection of society in that it internalizes within the individual the notions that society has about what the individual should and should not do. Since the id is seen as asocial with very little relation to external reality, its demands often run counter to the requirements of the ego and the superego. Observed behavior is considered by the psychoanalyst as a result of the outcome of this conflict.

A fourth point of view, which is most consistent with the view put forth in this book, sees between the individual and society an interactive relationship, in which neither is all-pervasive nor are the two in conflict. Rather the two forces complement each other and work together in the determination of man's behavior. Biological factors, for example, provide the individual with the potential for a certain range of behavior, but just where within that range he will in fact act is determined by social forces. To account for the way a particular athlete accomplishes a certain feat we start with the recognition that he is endowed with certain physical characteristics needed for the performance. However, this is not enough. We must know something about the society in which he lives in order to understand why he is engaging in this type of behavior in the first place, and we would probably need to know something about the patterns of interaction that he has had with others in order to explain why he gave up other pleasures to practice, exercise, and engage in the various acts needed to prepare him for his final athletic accomplishment.

These four ways of conceiving of the relationship between the individual and society are portrayed graphically in Figure 1. Society as a conglomeration of predisposed individuals, individuals molded completely by a preexisting society, society's demands and individual needs conflicting to determine the individual's behavior, and, finally, society's requirements and individual needs seen as interacting to determine behavior. This discussion falls far short of a review of the four differing theories of social psychology. We have briefly described these differing points of view to put into perspective the one approach that we are going to use in this book. The student should be clear that there are many other ways of viewing the relationship between man and society.

SOCIETY

It should be clear from the outset that, from our point of view, society and the individual cannot be dealt with independently of one another. Society is made up of individuals, and every individual is part of a society. *Society* can be seen as *a complex, yet organized set of relations in which individuals can act cooperatively*. The organized set of relations takes the form of role differentiations, or agreed-upon sets of expecta-

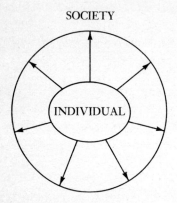

a. Society as a conglomeration
of predisposed individuals
(instinct theories).

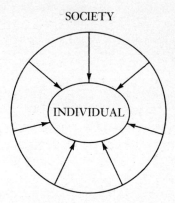

b. Individuals molded completely
by a preexisting society
(cultural determinism).

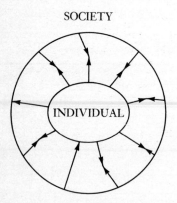

c. Societal forces compete and
conflict with inborn needs
(psychoanalytic theory).

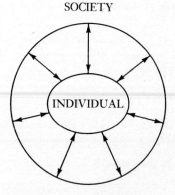

d. Interaction of societal influences and individual potential
(interactionist theories).

**Figure 1   Views of the relationship between the individual and
society.**

tions for persons holding particular positions within the set of relations. It also involves common attitudes and meanings such as those necessary for the application of any language. This does not necessarily mean common behavior. It does imply that these relationships, expectations, and common attitudes have emerged out of the interaction process through communication and learning.

Of course, this brief definition and description of society is misleading when applied to modern industrial society, for it does not reveal the complexity of such a society. In this respect, it is not too meaningful to try to analyze society as a whole, but rather one must look for more manageable units to study. Sociologists frequently handle this problem by dealing with the major social institutions of the society.

Social Institutions

An *institution* refers to *those systems of social relationships within society that embody the ultimate values of man and take the form of persistent norms and values that are oriented around the fulfillment of the basic needs of society.* Thus, assuming that the bearing and rearing of children are needs of society, we would say that those lasting customs and practices, values, and attitudes that develop around the fulfillment of these needs would make up the institution we commonly call the family. The customs governing dating; marriage and sex; the roles of the father, mother, and child; and the values placed on the maintenance of the marriage relationship all are part of the familial institution in America.

Institutional analyses start with the premise that there exist certain needs for the establishment and maintenance of any society and that around these needs will inevitably develop sets of relations and values, which we have termed institutions. Because a society must replenish its membership, procreation becomes a basic need, and the institution we called the family exists in every society. In order to transmit the culture to the new members of society, the educational institution arises. The economic institution consists of that system of social relationships within society that is oriented around the production, distribution, and consumption of goods and services. The cultural system of society directly concerned with the enforcement of behavior norms considered vital to maintenance of society is called the political institution. It includes the planning and coordination of activities for the general welfare of the members of society as well as the determining of who shall be accorded power in government and when and how it should be accorded. The religious institution establishes systems of morals, ethics, and attitudes toward the supernatural. Most sociologists and anthropologists agree that the institutions of the family, education, religion, economics, and government exist in some form in every society.

More recently, other factors have been recognized as necessary for the survival of large complex societies such as ours. These too might be called institutions. Various aspects of recreation, mass communication, transportation, health, and the like, might well be considered as institutions within our society.

When we speak of institutions, we are referring to the norms, customs, practices, attitudes, and values that are oriented around the fulfillment of a society's needs. So if we speak of mass communication as an institution, we are referring to the ways whereby information and entertainment are transmitted, including publication and distribution of daily newspapers; television programing; the gathering, editing, and broadcasting of the "news"; the laws and regulations governing the media; and the value placed on their operation.

Social Organization

It should be apparent from the above that life in modern society is extremely complex. However, it is just as apparent that it is patterned in a systematic organized fashion. There are standard ways of doing things. Behavior is motivated and constrained by the necessity to cooperate, which exists within every society. As persons relate to one another over a period of time they begin to develop organized ways of responding and corresponding expectations for the responses of others. Of course, we realize that an individual is born into an already existing society, where most of the patterns of expectations have been established for him. The customs of our society, its language, and its habits are all part of its social organization. So when, as social psychologists, we wish to understand human behavior, one of our first tasks is to understand the underlying organization that determines the expectations the members of society have for themselves and others. Human social formations vary tremendously. Some are short-lived and flexible, as in the case of two persons who meet for the first time, exchange ideas, and separate. Other organizations, as in the case in institutions, are formal and last over generations.

Norms

A valuable tool for unscrambling the complexities of modern society is the concept of *social norms*, which are *the rules or standards for behavior that are shared by the members of the group or the society*. Elsewhere in the book we will discuss group norms; here we are concerned with norms as the way persons are *expected* to behave as members of society. Norms can range from simple etiquette to complex laws. Since not all persons behave just as they are expected to, society develops what are called sanctions, or responses to deviant behavior that tend to force the deviant back toward conformity. Sanctions, too, vary considerably—a frown directed at the person who uses the wrong utensil and imprisonment of the criminal who commits a serious crime, are both examples of sanctions.

The process whereby the rules of proper and improper behavior (that is, norms) are learned by the new members of

society is called socialization. The young child is socialized
through his contacts with his family, his peers, his school, and
all other representatives of society with whom he comes into
contact as he grows up. He is taught what will be expected of
him as he becomes a member of society. This important process will be discussed in detail in a later chapter.

In dealing with the broad and encompassing concept of
norms, it has proved useful to introduce additional concepts to
handle the complexities. *Those norms that refer to expectations for individuals because of some characteristic that an
individual possesses or a position he holds in the group or
society* are called *roles.* For example, when we speak of the
role of the male in American society, we are referring to those
sets of expectations that society places on an individual who is
recognized as possessing the characteristic of being male. In
our society, we learn that the male is expected to perform
certain acts of etiquette such as holding a door for a woman,
he is expected to show certain personality traits (for example,
aggressiveness) and to dress in a particular way that differentiates him from women, and so forth. These role expectations
take many forms. Sometimes they are *rights* and *privileges,*
while at other times they are *duties* and *obligations.*

Of course, role analysis is not always simple and straightforward. Anyone who is aware of the concerns of the
women's liberation movement will know that the expectations
for males used in the example above are not held by all
members of society. These women are saying that the expectations of society are not inherently tied to the biological
characteristic (of being male) and that the society might be
improved if some of the expectations were changed. For the
male, this conflict in expectation may lead to confusion and
discomfort at times.

There are some positions in society that seem by their very
nature to lead to conflict. The position of the foreman in
industry is frequently used as an example of role conflict. This
arises because different sectors of his social environment have

different expectations for him. His fellow workers expect him to be concerned with their rights and needs, while the management that has made him foreman expects him to put the needs of the company first. When the expectations from one sector are incompatible with the expectations from other sectors, we have what we call role conflict. This is discussed in more detail in a later chapter.

Culture

Culture is usually thought of as the total ways of behaving, feeling, and thinking that are learned by man as a member of society. Social norms are at the very core of culture. They define for the members of society what is considered proper conduct. However, "culture" is a more encompassing term than "norms." Culture incorporates norms, roles, social institutions, organizations, and groups into what we might call *styles of life.* In the study of American culture, we would be interested in the life styles of the individuals within the society, which are consequences of its institutions, norms, and role expectations and the various dimensions of its social organizations.

Social Stratification

Of course, society is not made up of a simple homogeneous collection of individuals. Because of differing characteristics and experiences, individuals find themselves occupying differing positions within society—some are rich and some poor, some are white and some black, some are old and some young, and so on—and, through a long process of interaction and exchange, various values and expectations have been placed on the incumbents of these positions. Perhaps the most pervasive status system in American society is that which we call social class. An American's social class goes a long way in determining his specific social environment and the power and freedom he has in dealing with that environment.

Membership in the lower class in American society today

means far more than simply being poor—that is, lacking money. In coping with the problems that are shared by poor persons in an affluent society, the members of the lower class try various solutions, some of which become firmly established and are transmitted to successive generations.

The analysis of social stratification frequently leads to the conclusion that modern society might well be seen as a series of subsocieties, each with its separate norms, roles, and institutions, each with its unique way of coping with the problems brought about by its particular position in the larger society. Sociological analysis of the lower class demonstrates this further. Several studies have described the lower-class family as being matriarchal with serial monogamy. This means that the family is oriented around the mother who, with her children, holds together the home. The father-husband position is transient, with different men filling the role from time to time. This can be understood as a way of coping with the social environment when it is recognized that in lower-class areas unemployment is high and work (domestic, housekeeping, and the like) and public assistance both are more easily obtainable for women than for men. Religion among the lower class is likely to emphasize fate or luck, with an importance placed on a glorious life after death, thus providing a justification for the lowly lot of the persons here on earth and a reason for coping with the drudgeries of this life so as to arrive prepared for the life to come.

Formal education in our society has long been recognized as a middle-class establishment. No one knows this better than the lower-class child who is compelled to attend public school. If he is from the extreme lower end of the scale, he is likely to start his schooling without ever having seen a color crayon, with no knowledge that books exist, except perhaps comic books, and with no awareness that there is more to his name than "Bobby." At school, he encounters the middle-class boy who has been exposed to books since he was two years old, who has learned to read primer prose, and who can write his first *and* last name. Moreover, he must deal with a teacher who has a middle-class background, who has not been trained to deal with his problems, and who tends to divide her time and energy between controlling the lower-class children and teaching the bright, quiet, middle-class children. For the lower-class child, the real educational institution is not the schools, as it is for the middle-class child, but rather the street, where he learns the norms and values of the lower-class society. Note that not a small portion of his education consists of learning how to deal with middle-class institutions, which tend to impose their values on the lower class. One analysis of the concerns of the lower class claims that the major preoccupation of lower-class persons is with "trouble"—getting into and staying out of trouble.[1] Again, we can see this as a way of coping with political institutions that would impose middle-class rules and regulations on the lower class.

We have gone into some detail in discussing social class to show how the complexities of society have a different meaning for the individual depending upon his position or positions in society. Social class is only one dimension upon which we stratify the members of society. Race makes up another important dimension as do one's age, sex, and some other factors.

Let us now recall the definition of society given earlier in this chapter—society is an organized set of relations in which individuals can act cooperatively. It should now be possible to have some conception of what this statement—"organized set of relations"—entails when dealing with a complex system such as American society. These relations involve the differentiation of individuals into strata according to their positions or characteristics. They include the definitions of behavior as proper or improper, and they encompass the establishment of long-standing modes of coping with the problems of complex life. The organizational aspect of the definition refers to the

[1] Walter B. Miller, "Lower-Class Culture as a Generating Milieu of Gang Delinquency," *Journal of Social Issues*, vol. 14, no. 3, pp. 5-19, 1958.

way the society is put together in terms of social institutions and organizations that fulfill the needs of society while providing stability and consistency for the individual members. Into this complex system every individual is born, and in terms of this system he must cope and adjust if he is to become a normal human being.

THE INDIVIDUAL

We can deal with the individual outside the social context only as an abstraction, since no individual does, or can, so exist. However, it is valuable to look at some of the biological and physical factors that limit the impact of social influences. The newborn infant comes into the world equipped with certain biologically determined needs (such as the need for food and air). In addition, he has inherited certain cognitive, emotional, motor, and sensory potentials that permit him to be stimulated, and to a limited extent to respond, although the response is likely to be in the form of gross sounds and movements and to be more random than directed. Finally, his biological heritage determines his sex, race, somatotype, and to some extent his stature. However, the social significance of these characteristics is learned through his interaction with his social environment.

Biological factors are important for an understanding of the behavior of individuals, not by themselves but in their interaction with other factors. The individual's inherited physical and intellectual capacities might be seen as determining the limits on the accomplishments that the individual is capable of learning. But the actual level of attainment exhibited by the person is contingent on the various features of his social environment.

Immediately upon birth, social influences begin to mold the individual. The human infant starts with these biological potentials and builds through his experience with both his physical and social world, so that the individual we observe in his adult stage of life is a consequence of all three elements interdependently interwoven.

When the social psychologist observes the individual in a social setting he sees him as having certain acquired dispositions, such as attitudes, sentiments, conditioned responses, and the like, which have become a part of him over the years of interaction among these basic factors of life. The individual seen in this context is unique, since his particular combination of biological potential, physical experiences, and social experiences could not possibly be duplicated by any other human being.

This unique individual confronts the complex modern society. To understand the consequent behavior is the challenge of social psychology. In the next chapter we will deal with the process of social interaction in an attempt to explain the dynamics of the exchanges between individuals that provide the foundation for societal influence on the individual.

SUMMARY

The relationship between the individual and society is basic to social psychology. Some social psychologists have made society the all-prevailing factor in accounting for man's behavior. Others have suggested that its prime source of motivation is from within the individual. Still others have seen inner motivations conflicting with societal demands, and yet others see the two factors—society and the individual—interacting to account for man's behavior. This book takes the latter position.

In order to understand how society affects the individual, we need to have some overview of what a society is like. It can be seen in terms of its institutions, organization, norms, culture, and stratification. Likewise, the individual can be seen as a biological entity of great complexity. It is the theme of this book that neither the individual nor society can be completely comprehended without an understanding of how the two interrelate.

SUGGESTED REFERENCES

* Argyle, Michael: *The Psychology of Interpersonal Behavior*, Penguin Books Inc., Baltimore, 1967.
An English psychologist looks at interpersonal behavior.

* Benedict, Ruth: *Patterns of Culture* (1st ed., 1934), World Publishing Company, New York, 1949 (Mentor Books). An excellent example of how this well-known anthropologist sees the relationship between the individual and society.

Bierstedt, Robert: *The Social Order*, 3d ed., McGraw-Hill Book Company, New York, 1970.
Primarily a text for introductory sociology. Presents an excellent discussion of the relationship between man and society as seen by a sociologist.

* Brenner, Charles: *An Elementary Textbook of Psychoanalysis*, Doubleday & Company, Inc., Garden City, N.Y., 1955 (Anchor Books).
A clear and concise statement of the main features of the Freudian psychoanalytic approach.

Davis, Kingsley: *Human Society*, The Macmillan Company, New York, 1949.
Sophisticated yet readable presentation and analysis of the concept of society. Current despite being published more than twenty years ago.

* Hall, Calvin S.: *A Primer of Freudian Psychology*, World Publishing Company, New York, 1954 (Mentor Books).
A quick and easy way to get a good understanding of the basics of Freudian psychology.

* Inkeles, Alex: *What Is Sociology?* Prentice-Hall, Inc., Englewood Cliffs, N.J., 1964.
Good statement of sociologist's view of society.

Lindesmith, Alfred R., and Anselm L. Strauss: *Social Psychology*, 3d ed., Holt, Rinehart & Winston, Inc., New York, 1968.

Textbook in social psychology. Presents a complete statement of the symbolic interactionist approach.

* Manis, Jerome G., and Bernard N. Meltzer (eds.): *Symbolic Interaction: A Reader in Social Psychology*, 2d ed, Allyn & Bacon Inc., Boston, 1972.
  A collection of both classic essays and current research using the symbolic interactionist approach.

* Wallace, Anthony F. C.: *Culture and Personality*, Random House, Inc., New York, 1961.
  An anthropologist applies psychological principles to the study of culture and personality.

* Warner, W. Lloyd: *American Life: Dream and Reality*, rev. ed., The University of Chicago Press, Chicago, 1962.
  An assessment of the fluid American society and the impact of the advance of technology.

  Williams, Robin M., Jr.: *American Society*, 3d ed., Alfred A. Knopf, Inc., New York, 1970.
  One of the best descriptions of American middle-class society. A very readable and worthwhile book.

* References marked with asterisk are available in paperback.

FOUR

COMMUNICATION, LANGUAGE, AND PERCEPTION

The basic elements of human interaction are communication, language, and
perception. These form the foundation
necessary for any human relationship.
They must be understood before we can
move to any of the other social psychological concepts.

COMMUNICATION

In order to understand the process of
social interaction and how this interaction affects the individuals involved, we
should have some understanding of the
process of communication. For our purpose, we will use the concept of *communication* to refer to the *interchange of
meanings between people through the use
of symbols*. The word "symbol" refers to
anything that is intentionally used to
stand for something else. The symbols
most frequently used by human beings
are words. We will use the word "meaning" here in a rather broad sense to refer
to the entire set of ideas, images, feelings,
and action tendencies evoked by a symbol. When symbols are put together with
the intention of using them to transmit an
idea, we call them a message.

Figure 2 portrays the dynamics of the simplest form of communication. Person A, the source, has an idea (or image, feeling, or the like), which he wishes to convey to Person B, the destination. He puts his idea in the form of a message by using symbols (probably words) that evoke in him the idea he has in his mind. The message, now in the form of sound waves, hits on the eardrum of the destination, who decodes the symbols into ideas of his own. It should be clear from this simple analysis that *communication can take place only insofar as the two participants share common meanings of the symbols being used.* That is, communication takes place insofar as Idea 1 in Figure 2 is the same as or similar to Idea 2. If I say to you, "Please open the window," and if you, on hearing these words (symbols), get the idea that I am asking you to shut the door, then, of course, we are not communicating. For some reason, the symbols "Please open the window" do not have the same *meaning* for you as they do for me. However, there is no need that we have identical images in order for communication

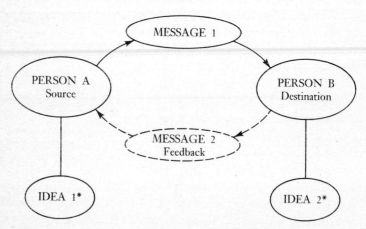

*Idea, image, feeling, or action tendency in the individual's mind

Figure 2   Two-person communication model.

to take place. I might have had the image of you climbing on a chair to open a window, while your image was one of standing on your tiptoes to accomplish the same thing. The difference in our images does not substantially affect the communication.

So far, our definition and explanation for communication is relatively simple and straightforward and for that reason may be misleading. The process of communication in interpersonal relationships is very complex, and the above analysis must be seen only as a starting point for a more complete analysis of the subject.

The model presented so far suggests that communication is a simple, one-directional phenomenon that proceeds from one person to another. However, a closer look at our definition shows that communication refers to the *interchange* of meanings. This means that the exchange goes in both directions. In Figure 2, the dotted lines suggest a message going back in the other direction from the destination to the source. In the simple two-person communication, if this return message provides evidence to the source that his original message got across, we call this *feedback*. Feedback is very important in an ongoing interactional setting. If, in response to my statement "Open the window," you get up and close the door, your act becomes a feedback message to me telling me that communication did not take place. However, had you stood up and closed the window I would probably conclude that you did get the message and that we were in communication.

To complicate our analysis even further, we must take into consideration that this process is part of an ongoing situation that takes place over time and cannot be viewed simply as a single act or unit. People come to share common understandings (communicate), not by one exchange, but by a whole series of exchanges, which take place within a social context and which only gradually lead to consensus. Consensus is the outcome of effective communication. It is the sharing of perspectives among those engaged in cooperative action. It does not happen all at once but is rather the result of an ongoing process that is built up, sustained, and reinforced through a continuing interchange of symbols or gestures. In the language of our earlier discussion, we must have feedback on the feedback on the feedback, and so on, before consensus can be approached. In the example used above, as you get up to open the window you look to me for confirmation and say by your look (but without words), "Am I doing as you asked?" I respond by a nod of my head.

Consensus is seldom, if ever, complete. An area of uncertainty usually remains, and around this area of uncertainty a large portion of the interchange takes place. If we leave the simplistic example of the window and imagine a more complex situation, it may become more obvious. Say that after class one day you and a friend are discussing your impression of one of your instructors. It is likely to be an ongoing interchange—your evaluative judgments backed with examples interspersed with his responses of confirmation or requests for clarification. With each exchange of messages, the uncertainties are reduced, which enables your friend to respond with greater confidence. It seems safe to say that in most instances, communication is a continuous process.

LANGUAGE

Our study of communication assumed the existence of what we call *language—the system of verbal or written symbols that are shared with some degree of consistency by the members of a community*. The anthropologists tell us that all human societies have languages. At the same time, evidence indicates that they are not found in any subhuman species. Of all the factors that distinguish man from lower animals, man's ability to manipulate higher-order symbols (that is, to use language) is perhaps the most basic and most profound in accounting for the differences between man and animal.

This can be seen most distinctly when we consider the central role of language in man's most significant accomplishments. For example, the accumulation and transmission of culture require language. Dogs and monkeys can learn to respond to signals and, on occasion, can be taught rather complicated tricks; however, each dog, or each new generation of dogs, must be taught the same way and nothing accumulates. But through the use of language it is possible for the human being to experience secondhand. That is, it is possible for man, by using symbols, to describe a situation and thus evoke in others the response that would be expected from a firsthand experience. Thus, experiences can be stored, history can be transmitted, and a culture is made possible.

The accumulative benefits of language shape the difference between man and animal. An animal transmits to its offspring approximately the same things today that its ancestors did 1,000 years ago. By comparing man over the same period one can see the effects of language and culture.

Some authors have clarified this point by introducing the term "sign" to refer to any cue that has come to stand for something else.[1] Sign behavior can range from an animal coming when a whistle is blown to your listening to a lecture. Signs may take the form of a siren that stands for fire, a smell that means breakfast is cooking, a meter that tells you how fast you are driving, a clenched fist that symbolizes a revolutionary movement, a cross that is a symbol of religious beliefs, and so on. Words are the most versatile signs, for there are vast possibilities in manipulating them. We can experience the things that the words stand for whether or not they are present, or whether they are in the past, the future, or only in our imagination.

It is valuable to conceive of three elements of sign behav-

---

[1] Alfred R. Lindesmith and Anselm L. Strauss, *Social Psychology*, 3d ed., Holt, Rinehart & Winston, Inc., New York, 1968. The discussion that follows relies heavily on Chapter 2 in Lindesmith and Strauss.

ior—the sign, what it signifies, and the interpreter. We should not confuse the sign with the thing that it stands for. The interpreter is the one who makes the connection between the sign and its referent.

Signs can be classified as conventional or natural. A natural sign is a stimulus that is perceived to have a direct connection with something else for which it becomes a sign. The sign and its referent consistently occur together in the same space-time framework. The smell of bacon comes to stand for breakfast since the two occur together in the same approximate space-time sequence. By contrast, the conventional sign derives its meaning from social consensus and can be seen as having a degree of arbitrariness about it. The reason that the word "cow" stands for a four-legged animal that gives milk has nothing to do with the intrinsic value of the word, but rather because in our society we have *agreed* to use the word for this purpose. This is demonstrated by the fact that the many languages that exist in our world have many different words to stand for the same four-legged creature. There is nothing about the cow herself that requires that she be called a cow.

A conventional sign then becomes synonymous with the word symbol as we have used it earlier in this chapter. It becomes the focus of our concern as we delve into the problems of language. Lindesmith and Strauss,[2] who present one of the most careful analyses of this subject, suggest that there are three important characteristics of language symbols that distinguish them from other kinds of signs:

1. They constitute systems so that the meaning of any single symbol cannot be grasped in isolation, but must be understood within the system. For examples: "wife," which is intelligible only in terms of a wider linkage of symbols like "husband," "marriage," and the like.

2. Language symbols, as we shall soon show, are inherently

[2] *Ibid.*, p. 33.

social in character and meaning. They evoke from the person who produces or uses them the same or similar responses as those elicited from the persons to whom they are directed. If communication is faulty or if the speaker talks past the listener, the words do not function as symbols.

3. They can be produced voluntarily even when the external events or objects to which they refer are absent or nonexistent. We may thus say that although people carry their symbolic systems around with them, the fact that one makes assertions about an object does not prove that the object is present or even that it exists.

Still a further aspect of language needs to be considered. Note that the symbols that we use seldom refer to a specific concrete object, feeling, or event. Rather they refer to a class of objects. The word "dog" refers to a class of animals and it enables its user to differentiate between dogs and cats, dogs and people, and so on. However, it does not discriminate between a collie and a German shepherd. Words then are *abstractions*. The word "collie" is lower on the ladder of abstraction than the word "dog" in that "collie" refers to a narrower range of objects than does "dog." This is important in relating our discussion of language to what has been said about communication.

Going back to the model presented in Figure 2, we can identify the three elements of sign behavior mentioned above. First, the sign would be represented by Message 1. The thing that the sign stands for is Idea 1 and the interpreter is Person A. Now it is the task of Person A to translate the idea that he has in his mind into significant symbols, that is, symbols that mean the same for Person B as they do for him. This is the heart of good communication. How do you select symbols, arrange and present them so that they will convey to the listener the idea or image you wish to convey? You must select the proper level of abstraction. Too high a level may lead to too wide a range of possible ideas or images in the other person

e is not likely to convey the desired mean-
bitten by an animal," leaves the listener
type of animal might have bitten you. Or if
crete or too specific a word the listener may
with your specific reference. "I was just bitten
by Joe, be meaningless unless the listener knew that
Joe was your dog. So you say, "I was just bitten by a *dog*,"
which is high enough in the ladder of abstraction so that you
can be reasonably certain that your listener will share the
symbols used, but not so high as to make the message too
vague to be meaningful.

In addition to your selection of words, you may add gestures to be certain that your message is understood. A pained
look on your face and grabbing yourself where the dog bit
you would add to the effectiveness of the message. Further,
along with the accompanying gestures, you probably will
incorporate vocal intonations. These intonations are just one
more factor that go into the attempt to communicate. "I was
just bitten by a dog," if presented in a calm casual way,
without much in the form of accompanying gestures, could
convey the message that would read "I am simply informing
you of the fact that a dog bit me recently." However, with the
correct intonation and accompanying gestures, the same words
can be made to mean, "Help! A dog just bit me! I'm in pain
and in need of assistance." From this it should be clear that not
all communication takes the form of verbal symbols.

PERCEPTION

Perception is a term that *refers to the ways in which orga-
nisms respond to the stimuli picked up by their sense organs.*
Before we show the importance of this concept to the understanding of communication, let us look at some of the implications of the definition.

The two rather distinct steps in the process of perception

must be handled separately. First, there is the question of how
the physical object in the environment becomes implanted in
the organism. Second, we must deal with the question: Once it
is there what determines how the organism responds to it? The
first question has been handled by the physiological psychologists, who trace the mechanical processes involved. In the case
of visual perception, for example, they are likely to use an
analogy between the eye and a camera and discuss how the
light reflects from the object and reaches the eye, how the
light impinges on the retina of the eye, how the retina is
connected with the central nervous system, and how impulses
pass through the nerves. For our purposes, we shall call this the
process of "seeing" and leave its analysis to the physiological
psychologists. As social psychologists we are interested in the
second question: Once we see how do we perceive? That is,
how do we select out of all the stimuli that the sense organs
bring into the central nervous system certain ones to respond
to and others to ignore.

Think for a minute of all the stimuli that at this particular
moment are available to you by way of your sense organs—all
of the things within your range of vision, the sounds that
reach the ear, the things you are touching and feeling (both
inside and outside your body), those things you taste and
smell. Most of this must be ignored if you are going to function smoothly in the routines of living. The study of perception for the social psychologist is a study of the process of
selection or discrimination.

The analysis of this process might be divided into two parts:
What determines the selection and How is it accomplished? Let
us consider the "How" question first. Persons act in response
to the objects in their environment in terms of their classification of these objects. Categorization is an integral part of
human perception. As Lindesmith and Strauss[3] point out, "An

[3] *Ibid.*, p. 152.

object is perceived characteristically not as an isolated item but as a member of some class. Actually we see class representatives not bare and unnamed isolated objects." Note that this discussion is very similar to our earlier discussion of language. Language is a process of providing labels for classes of objects. Linguistic classifications, it turns out, are an integral part of the perceptual process. We learn that certain words or labels stand for a certain class of objects (or actions). This linguistic classification becomes the vehicle or tool we use to enable us to perceive the object; "objects cannot be perceived as class members unless the observer's language has already designated these classes or enables him to invent new categories." An example frequently used to elaborate this point is the Eskimos' linguistic devices for dealing with the phenomenon we call snow. It seems that the Eskimos have no word equivalent to our word "snow," but rather have a large number of words to refer to snow in various stages and conditions. This prompts a question: Does this fine discriminatory classification of snow make it possible for the Eskimos to make similarly fine perceptual distinctions? The answer is debatable; however, we do know that, with the elaborate language, the Eskimos can talk about the highly specialized condition and can respond quickly and consistently from one situation to the other. Although we cannot bring completely convincing evidence for our contention that language is essential for perception, there is little doubt that the existence of linguistic distinctions enhances perception by increasing the possibility that certain discriminations will be made.

So far, we have seen that perception is a process of discrimination of stimuli in terms of some classification scheme. In addition, we suggested that the linguistic devices that the individual had available to him influenced, if they did not determine, the range of perception possible. This does not go far enough. In some senses, we have described only *how* the process works but not what actually determines the perception. Many stimuli reach the sense organs, and we have linguistic categories potentially capable of classifying far more of them than we can possibly handle. Why are we sensitive to some while ignoring others?

Several factors determine this selectivity. Our *past experience* is an important factor. It sensitizes us to certain things; it gives them meaning beyond their physical existence, thus influencing our reaction. If we come across a person with a gun in one hand and an apple in the other, most of us are likely to perceive the gun first because our past experience with guns has given them special significance. Under this heading of past experience would be included all types of specialized experiences and training that would lead to different perceptions. The boy who grew up on a farm will perceive a tree in quite a different fashion than does the city boy. The medical doctor when he looks in your mouth perceives a quite different set of phenomena than you do when you look in the mirror.

In addition to the category of past experience, your *interest of the moment* will affect your perception. If you have just come from a course in anthropology you may well perceive what is presented in this book in a different fashion than if you had just come from a course in physiology. Our attention is given on a selective basis. For example, close your eyes for a moment and listen to the sounds around you. If you followed these instructions, your attention was drawn to something you had not been perceiving. Your interest of the moment was drawn away from reading the book and toward listening to sounds. Those sounds were there all along, but, since your interest of the moment was directed elsewhere, you did not perceive them until they were called to your attention.

A similar factor might be labeled the *condition of the organism*. Presence or absence of hunger, excitement, or fatigue can have important effects on what you perceive. A hungry person, when confronted with our man holding the gun and the apple, may perceive the apple long before he recognizes the presence of the gun.

Putting these factors together, it is easy to arrive at the

conclusion that we perceive what we are looking for. This is
not altogether true, but it certainly holds that a person's
perceptions will follow the lines of familiarities and expectations. One can see how this process influences the operation of
stereotypes. A stereotype usually refers to a set of characteristics, frequently derogatory, erroneously attributed to a class of
persons. The classic example is the stereotype held by the
racial bigot that Negroes are lazy. When a person holding this
stereotype comes upon a Negro sitting on a park bench he
"perceives" the Negro's behavior as laziness, thus seeing what
he expected to see and reinforcing his stereotype.

The fact that perception is affected by these many factors
sometimes leads to distorted perceptions in which stimuli are
misinterpreted or the same situation is perceived quite differently by different individuals. This should not lead us to forget
the fact that reality sets limits to perception. When a person
claims to see nonexistent objects like pink elephants he is
hallucinating, not perceiving. Perception is limited by what is
actually present in the environment.

Perception in social settings becomes extremely complex and
we will have to reserve some of our analysis for the following
chapter. At present let us consider one more example to
demonstrate the complexities of social perception and the role
that language plays in the process. Consider what is involved in
a store owner "seeing" a customer shoplifting from his store.
Actually, he does not see the person shoplift. What he sees is a
person putting an object in his pocket and leaving the store.
The customer's actions appear suspect, he is nervous and looks
from side to side. In the store owner's evaluation of the situation, he attributes to the person certain motives and intentions
and, thereby, is sensitized to these behavioral characteristics.
He cannot see the intentions; he infers them. In order for him
to perceive the shoplifting, he must define or interpret the act
as one of taking merchandise from a store without the intent
of paying; he must be aware of the fact that in his culture

people do not put objects in their pocket and leave the store, if they intend to pay for them; and he must put these together and make his conclusion. Phenomena that involve intent, motives, and expressions of feelings are frequently difficult to perceive. Without a common background of social experiences among the participants involved, accurate perception may become impossible.

How does perception affect communication? Figure 3 is an extension of the model presented in Figure 2, to include the analysis of perception in the communication process. It deals specifically with this question: What are the dynamics involved when an individual experiences an event and then communicates this experience to a second person? Starting at the top of the figure, we have the event that occurs in the external environment independent of the individual. Then through the physiological functioning of the sense organs this event, along with many others, is brought into the person's central nervous system. Now the process of perception operates, allowing him to sort through all the stimuli and pick out certain ones to respond to. He makes sense out of the situation by his classification of the objects or events. This demands learning and probably some linguistic devices. Now he has in his mind the image or idea that he wishes to communicate to the other person. Note that there is in our analysis a new and important ingredient that was not present in our earlier discussion of communication. In the process of perception, the individual has classified and assigned linguistic categories to the phenomena he now wishes to communicate. This act of perception may give the individual a start toward communication since the first step in communication requires that he classify the objects and code them in the form of a message. *The classification scheme that enables him to perceive the event may also be useful in enabling him to communicate the event.* The additional consideration in the communication situation concerns the other person. Does he (Person B in Figure 3)

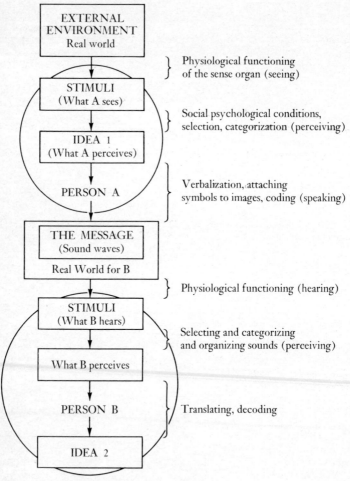

Figure 3   Perception and communication.

share the same past experiences, interests, and so on, to enable him to respond to the symbols that the initial individual (Person A) used in his perception? Person A may find it necessary to make some adjustment at this point.

Our model brings out another important relationship between perception and communication. Note that when the message leaves Person A, it is in the form of sound waves (and light waves that convey his gestures). These sound waves are the reality for Person B. Person B must decode, categorize, classify, and make sense out of them before we can say communication has taken place.

This long chain of processes leaves considerable possibility for distortion and confusion. However, with redundant repeating messages, accompanying gestures and vocal intonations, and extended feedback, we find that it is usually possible to communicate with satisfactory accuracy events that we experience. When an event is experienced by one person who transmits it to another, who in turn transmits it to a third person, and so on, the story almost certainly will be distorted in the process. We learn to be leery of secondhand or third-hand information—hearsay evidence is always suspect.

SUMMARY

In this chapter, we have dealt with some of the elementary forms of social interaction—communication, language, and perception. These processes are seen as the necessary conditions for the functioning of the more complex interactional processes of role-taking and the development of the self-concept, which will be discussed in the next chapter. All these processes assume the preexistence of certain skills on the part of the individual and certain forms within the society. In Chapter 3 we briefly discussed the structure of society into which the individual is born. A later chapter on socialization will discuss the acquisition of the skills needed by the individual to perceive, to communicate, and to take roles.

SUGGESTED REFERENCES

* Berelson, Bernard, and Gary A. Steiner: *Human Behavior*, shorter
ed. Harcourt Brace Jovanovich, Inc., New York, 1967.
Chapters 7 through 12 have a readable, well-documented presentation of communication, perception, and related topics.

* Brown, Roger: *Words and Things*, The Free Press, New York,
1958.
An excellent introduction to the study of language.

* Church, Joseph: *Language and the Discovery of Reality*, Random
House, Inc., New York, 1961 (Vintage Books).
A highly readable and informative account of the way human
beings come to discover reality.

Duncan, Hugh D.: *Communication and Social Order*, Oxford
University Press, New York, 1962.
A symbolic interactionist's analysis of language and com-
munication.

* Hall, Edward T.: *The Silent Language*, Doubleday & Company,
Inc., Garden City, N.Y., 1959 (paperback: Fawcett World
Library, Premier Books, New York).
A widely read treatment of how people "talk" to each other
without the use of words.

Hertzler, Joyce O.: *A Sociology of Language*, Random House,
Inc., New York, 1965.
Comprehensive scholarly analysis of the reciprocal relationship
between language and society. Deals particularly with the function of language.

Lindesmith, Alfred R., and Anselm L. Strauss: *Social Psychology*,
3d ed., Holt, Rinehart & Winston, Inc., New York, 1968.
One of the best presentations of the role of language in the explanation of human social behavior.

Morris, Charles W.: *Signs, Language and Behavior*, Prentice-Hall
Inc., Englewood Cliffs, N.J., 1946.

An attempt to develop a conceptual scheme for the systematic study of all symbol behavior. A classic in the study of language.

* Pierce, J. D.: *Symbols, Signs and Noise,* Harper & Row, Publishers, New York, 1961 (Harper Torchbook).
A sophisticated analysis of the nature and process of communication.

* Ross, Ralph: *Symbols and Civilization,* Harcourt Brace Jovanovich, Inc., New York, 1962.
Describes how human civilization creates and, in turn, is created by its common symbolic heritage.

* Segall, Marshall, Donald Campbell, and Melville J. Herskovits: *The Influence of Culture on Visual Perception,* The Bobbs-Merrill Co. Inc., Indianapolis, 1966.
A report of a series of cross-cultural studies on differences in visual perception. Excellent example of the application of rigid research methods to important conceptual problems.

Shibutani, Tamotsu: *Society and Personality,* Prentice-Hall, Inc., Englewood Cliffs, N.J., 1961.
One of the best presentations of communication from an interactionist perspective.

Vetter, Harold: *Language Behavior and Communication,* F. E. Peacock Publishers, Inc., Itasca, Ill., 1969.
A simple introduction to theory and research in language communication.

* References marked with asterisk are available in paperback.

FIVE

INTERACTION PROCESSES: ROLE-TAKING AND THE SELF-CONCEPT

In the last chapter, when we discussed communication and perception, we were concerned with the skills needed for meaningful social exchange. In this chapter, we move a step further and consider just what processes operate once we can make the assumption that the individual has learned a language, knows how to perceive his environment, and can communicate his experiences. Role-taking is an interactional process whereby the individual learns to choose the forms of behavior expected of him by others. Within this interactional exchange, the individual develops a conception of himself that functions to direct his behavior. Understanding these two concepts is crucial to a comprehension of the way the individual is influenced by those about him.

THINKING

Although we cannot in a book of this scope go into the intricacies of the functioning of the mind, it is possible to suggest some dimensions of its operation that are useful in understanding the interaction process. George Herbert Mead,[1] whose thinking strongly influenced the discussion in this chapter, has suggested that the process of mental activity involves, at least in part, selecting appropriate solutions from a series of alternatives that the mind places before the organism. More explicitly, when the individual is faced with a problem—that is, when he cannot rely on habit but must consciously deliberate—he can use his linguistic skills to conjure up in his mind a number of alternative solutions and choose among these alternatives before he actually acts. Mead uses the example of an individual who is walking along and comes upon a mud puddle. Up to this point, he could rely on habit to tell him where to place his feet. However, the mud puddle requires some conscious deliberation. He starts the process of considering alternatives—seeing himself (in his mind's eye) walking into the puddle and getting wet. He rejects this alternative and considers jumping. He continues imagining and rejecting until he comes up with a solution that is satisfactory. Then, and only then, does he act. Of course, he learns to produce and consider these alternatives in rapid sequence so chances are that, from the time he first sees the mud puddle until he actually reaches it, he has had time to consider four or five alternatives and to come up with one that is satisfactory.

This is by no means solely a matter of trial and error, for the selections considered are from his past experience and he is continually building a repertory of responses. The next day when he comes to the puddle, he will need considerably less deliberation, and in a few days he will get by completely on the basis of habit.

We learn to go through rather complex operations relying almost completely on habit. Consider driving a car with a stick

[1] George Herbert Mead, *Mind, Self and Society*, The University of Chicago Press, Chicago, 1934, part II.

shift. Shifting gears requires the coordination of hands, feet, and eyes; but a person who has been driving for any length of time can accomplish this task easily without thinking (that is, without conscious awareness of what he is doing).

Of course, during the time no conscious consideration is needed to get us through the routines of life, the mind is still quite active. According to Mead, we are continually working on hypothetical problems, or problems we might anticipate meeting in the future. So when our walker gets beyond the mud puddle he does not need his mind to tell him which foot to put down first. He can think about something else. Maybe he is thinking about calling his girl for a date that night. Again, he will conjure up alternative ways to approach this problem and get the results he wants.

ROLE-TAKING

When the individual is confronted with another person rather than a simple object like a mud puddle, the situation becomes much more complex. We are now dealing with a social situation or what Mead called the social act. Now, in order for the person to present himself with useful alternatives he must be able to anticipate the responses of the other person to his behavior. He accomplishes this by a process we call role-taking. *Role-taking is one of the most important concepts in social psychology and refers to the process of putting one's self in the place of the other (in one's mind) and responding to oneself as it is felt the other will respond.* In other words, in your imagination, you get into the shoes of the other person and look at yourself as an object. This can be done only because you have developed the linguistic skills that enable you to perform the elaborate operation of choosing between mentally contrived alternatives. By way of illustration, assume you intend to go to your instructor and see if you can get the grade on your last exam changed from a C to a B. Long before you reach his office, you begin to rehearse taking roles. In your mind's eye, you see yourself approach the instructor and ask him boldly, "Why in hell did you give me such a low grade?" Now, still in your mind, you move into his seat and see yourself making such a statement. By taking his view, you try to anticipate how he will respond. Thinking him to be a pillar in a fundamentalist church, you may imagine him throwing you out of his office. Since this is not the end you wish to accomplish, you abandon that alternative and go on to another. You continue this process until you hit upon one that seems likely to be effective. Note that instructors are much more difficult to predict than mud puddles, so your task is much more difficult. When you arrive at his door, you may have a set approach that you have decided upon. Then, in response to your knock, a gruff voice yells, "What do you want?" This did not fit the picture you had constructed of your instructor, and all your earlier role-taking has to be revised. However, a good role-taker can adjust with considerable speed, and chances are by the time you have the door open you have considered several new alternatives, now using the additional cues you received from his response to your knock.

In the interpersonal situation, role-taking is continuous. The images of the other are being revised as additional evidence is gained from your perceptions of his actual responses. But remember, role-taking is the process that goes on in the mind. One never learns the accuracy of his anticipations of how the other person would have responded to those alternatives rejected. He gets feedback only on the one course of action that he finally decides upon.

ROLE-TAKING ABILITY

The individual's skill in anticipating the responses of others is crucial in determining how well he will operate in social situations. The ability to get outside one's self and to take the role of the other and accurately anticipate how the other will respond to his actions is called *role-taking ability*. Role-taking skills vary in several ways. In some situations, the persons involved seem to clearly understand each other's perceptions and attitudes, and their interaction goes smoothly. In other settings, persons involved appear to be quite out of touch with each other, and misunderstandings and confusion run rampant. Below we will consider in a somewhat systematic fashion the factors that determine the accuracy of an individual's role-taking in an interpersonal situation.

Familiarity with the "Other"

This familiarity can take two forms: (1) familiarity with the specific other and (2) awareness of the characteristics of the other individual and familiarity with behavioral correlates of these characteristics. In the first instance, we are suggesting that one learns by exposure to the particular individual. After you have interacted with an individual over a period of time, you become familiar with his responses and are better able to anticipate what his responses might be to the alternative actions you are contemplating. You will take roles better with a friend with whom you have interacted frequently than with a stranger whom you meet for the first time.

The second form of familiarity with the other is the situation in which the other displays characteristics with which you are familiar and that aid in anticipating his responses to you. When you are confronted face-to-face with an individual, even though he may be a stranger whom you have never seen before, that person will provide you with clues as to the type of person he is and this evidence may well aid you in role-taking. Usually, you can see what his sex is, his approximate age, his race, and, frequently from his attire, you can get some clue as to what he does for a living. Does it help to know that the person you are confronted with is a white girl in her early twenties who is probably a student? You will probably answer yes, because you are familiar with some of the behavioral correlates of these characteristics. You know enough about the characteristic of sex to know that if you approach a person to ask for a date the response would vary considerably depending on that person's sex. The same thing operates for the other characteristics. You would probably expect different responses to your request for a date from a young girl than from an elderly lady, a black girl than a white girl, a secretary than a student. Of course, we are not always correct either in our perception of the characteristics of the other or the behavior we guess to be a correlate of these characteristics. What we are suggesting here is that *in general* the more we know about the other, either through firsthand interactional experience or through familiarity with his characteristics the better we will be able to take roles with him.

Familiarity with the Social Situation

In a new and strange situation, the individual usually finds himself quite uncomfortable. He does not know what to expect or how to act. Even if he has some familiarity with the others in the setting, he may feel confused. Familiarity with the situation helps to improve role-taking. Let us go back to our example of the student who goes in to see his instructor about a change in his grade. The first factor we discussed above indicates that if he is familiar with the particular instructor, he might find his role-taking easier or if he is aware that he is confronted with a college professor and is familiar with the ways of professors, he might improve his role-taking. In this section we add another factor. How familiar is he with the situation? If he is the type that goes in after every exam and asks his instructor to raise his grade, he may have become very adept at anticipating how others will respond to his inquiries. Or more generally, he may have made a habit of always asking for a little more than he receives and thus may have built up an experience base that aids him in anticipating the responses of others in these situations. This is what we mean when we say that the more familiar the person is with the situation the better will be his role-taking ability.

Feedback Available

In an earlier section, we pointed out how communication improved with the interchange of ideas through feedback responses. The same thing occurs in role-taking settings, and to some degree the discussion of communication and the present discussion of role-taking are dealing with the same thing. As we act in relation to another person, that action is likely to be in terms of an attempt to transmit an idea to that person (communication). The feedback, or response, is what we have tried to anticipate by our role-taking. When the other responds in the way that we had anticipated, we conclude that our line of thinking was correct and feel that we are now more familiar with the individual and the situation. As the exchange continues, role-taking improves, and the interaction proceeds smoothly. Of course, we would not be led to believe that this is always the case. Sometimes a missed cue or feedback that is misread can throw the whole exchange off so that the longer the interaction, the greater the confusion and misunderstanding. However, it seems safe to say that in general the longer the interaction, the better the role-taking.

General Role-taking Ability

Here we are suggesting that independent of the familiarity with the other and the situation or of the feedback that is available, the individual brings into the situation a general ability to take roles. This individual attribute varies considerably within the population. Some persons appear to be extremely sensitive to others and to situations and cues and come out good role-takers in almost every situation. Others are singularly inept; they seem to be blind to the cues and ignorant of the characteristics of others and of the expectations for the situation. These are extremes and most of us fall somewhere between. It should not be assumed that we are talking here about simple intellectual ability, since, although there may be some correlation, it is not unusual to find an intellectual genius who is a poor role-taker or a person bordering on feeblemindedness who is quite adept at anticipating the roles of others.

It is valuable to ask where this general role-taking ability comes from. We reject the notion that some psychologists imply regarding intelligence, that role-taking skills are inherited. Rather we take the position that this skill develops through experience. A wide exposure to a variety of situations and persons will enhance the individual's role-taking skills.

Of particular importance in this development is an extended exposure of the child to his age-mates or peers. Recall that feedback available was listed as one of the factors that enhanced role-taking. We need to observe the responses of others to us to know how they are evaluating our actions so that we can anticipate future reactions. In adult life, at least in our society, those responses to our behavior are likely to be hidden behind a veil of politeness or inhibition. In other words, adults frequently hide their actual responses to our behavior and provide us with false feedback. Ask an associate how he likes your new tie or dress and you are likely to get a response like "It's very nice," which of course tells you nothing. Children have not developed these inhibitions; they are much more open in their responses and will "tell it like it is." To the adult, the child may seem brutally frank in his responses to his peers, but the other children are usually not offended and are gaining important experience in role-taking that will aid them in anticipating the responses of others later, when in adult life the direct feedback is missing or misleading. According to our contention, a child who grows up in an exclusively adult environment would have difficulty role-taking unless enough other factors compensate.

Encounter-group experiences sometimes operate in a fashion similar to that of childhood interaction. Frequently in the encounter group, members are instructed to lay aside their inhibitions and be completely open in their responses to others. This has the potential of helping the individual to better understand how others are responding to him.

Perceptual Factors

Since the interpersonal situation demands perceptual skills, anything that affects perception might also have an effect on role-taking. The person's past experience, his interest of the moment, or the conditions of his body would influence his ability to take roles in a particular situation.

We have listed the factors that seem most important in determining how well the person can put himself in the place of the other and anticipate what that other's response will be. Obviously, role-taking ability enhances communication and the smooth functioning of the social exchange. Now we can turn to another important function or consequence of role-taking and the interactional situation.

THE SELF-CONCEPT

As the individual is becoming a proficient role-taker, not only is he learning about others, but he is also learning about himself. By getting outside himself into the role of the other, he is able to look at himself as an object. This image he devises of himself we call his self-concept. More formally, we will define the *self-concept as that organization of qualities that the individual attributes to himself*. The self-concept is organized in the sense that the individual perceives himself as a unit, and the qualities that he attributes to himself are fitted together into a meaningful whole. These qualities take the form of both evaluative attributes, which are usually described by use of adjectives (handsome, ambitious, and the like), and role or position labels, usually expressed by nouns (child, doctor, and so forth). This should not be confused with self-esteem, which is a unidimensional concept referring to how highly the individual regards himself. The self-concept has many dimensions and might be seen as the individual's organization of *all* the qualities that are relevant to his self-evaluation.

Self-concept and Others

It is our contention that the self-concept results from social interaction. Charles Cooley,[2] a pioneer in social psychology, referred to the self-concept as the *looking-glass self*. Using the analogy of a mirror, he suggested that we learn about ourselves by observing the reflection of our behavior in the responses of others to us. George Herbert Mead[3] elaborated on this, insisting that it was only through this process of getting outside ourselves and perceiving ourselves as others do (according to our perception of others' responses to us) that we can get any idea about ourselves.

Perhaps this can be best understood by a look at the underlying assumptions that make up these notions of the emergence of the self and its effect on behavior.[4] The first, and most central to the discussion so far, is the proposition that (1) *the individual's conception of himself is based on his perception of the way others are responding to him.* A second proposition makes the study of the self-concept of particular importance for it asserts that (2) *the individual's conception of himself functions to direct his behavior* (defined broadly to include action, appearance, and so forth). Add to these two more obvious assumptions: (3) *the individual's perceptions of*

[2] Charles H. Cooley, *Human Nature and the Social Order*, Schocken Books, Inc., New York, 1964, chaps. 5 and 6.
[3] Mead, *op. cit.*, part III.
[4] The discussion that follows was introduced earlier in John W. Kinch, "A Formalized Theory of the Self-concept," *American Journal of Sociology*, vol. 68, no. 4, pp. 481–486, January, 1963.

others' responses are an accurate reflection of the actual responses that the others are directing toward the individual, and (4) *these actual responses are based on their (others') reaction to the individual's behavior.* If we put these four propositions or assumptions together we have what appears to be a circular model: The person's behavior determines others' responses to him, which are perceived by that individual, who in turn uses these perceptions to determine the conception he has of himself, which will be influential in determining how he will behave. This new behavior is again responded to and the process starts around again. This is shown graphically in Figure 4.

The story that follows will help to elaborate on the significance of this model in understanding the role of the self-concept in the interactive process.

A group of graduate students in a seminar in social psychology became interested in the notions implied in the interactionist approach. One evening after the seminar five of the male members

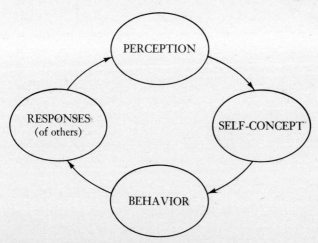

Figure 4 **Relationship between self and other.**

of the group were discussing some of the implications of the theory and came to the realization that it might be possible to invent a situation where the "other" systematically manipulated their responses to another person, thereby changing that person's self-concept and in turn his behavior. They thought of an experiment to test the notions they were dealing with. They chose as their subject (victim) the one girl in their seminar. The subject can be described as, at best, a very plain girl who seemed to fit the stereotype (usually erroneous) that many have of graduate student females. The boys' plan was to begin in concert to respond to the girl as if she were the best-looking girl on campus. They agreed to work into it naturally so that she would not be aware of what they were up to. They drew lots to see who would be the first to date her. The loser, under the pressure of the others, asked her to go out. Although he found the situation quite unpleasant, he was a good actor and by continually saying to himself "she's beautiful, she's beautiful . . ." he got through the evening. According to the agreement, it was now the second man's turn and so it went. The dates were reinforced by the similar responses in all contacts the men had with the girl. In a matter of a few short weeks the results began to show. At first it was simply a matter of more care in her appearance; her hair was combed more often and her dresses were more neatly pressed, but before long she had been to the beauty parlor to have her hair styled, and was spending her hard-earned money on the latest fashions in women's campus wear. By the time the fourth man was taking his turn dating the young lady, the job that had once been undesirable was now quite a pleasant task. And when the last man in the conspiracy asked her out he was informed that she was pretty well booked up for some time in the future. It seems there were more desirable males around than those "plain" graduate students.[5]

Does the story conform with the model presented in Figure 4? Presumably it does. Starting with the boys' responses to the young lady, these actions, although contrived and not based on

[5] *Ibid.*, pp. 482–483.

her actual behavior, did give the impression that the male students had intended; and she perceived these responses as indicative of the impression she was making on others. When this perception persisted, she found it necessary to change her conception of herself to come into line with this new set of reactions she was receiving. Eventually, it started to change her behavior.

At the end of our story the circle is complete, for the boys are now responding to the girl's behavior (in showing their desire to go out with this attractive young lady).

Of course, no meaningful theory can be entirely circular. However, this conceptualization appears to be a valid portrayal of the dynamics that operate in a social system once the action is under way. The model also provides an excellent framework to demonstrate how changes in the individual's self-concept came about. When one comes into a new group or confronts a new individual, he does not enter void of a conception of himself. He brings with him a conception of himself that he has built up over many social encounters and it is this self-concept that he uses as a guide for his initial behavior. In the most common situation, his action is responded to and perceived accurately by others. He perceives them as seeing him in about the way he sees himself, which has the consequence of reinforcing his earlier conception of himself.

Changes in the Self-concept

This should not lead us to the conclusion that once the self-concept is established it remains static. A person's conception of himself is dynamic and, like the girl's in the example, changes from time to time. However, it is stable enough so that it does not change with each response that is directed toward it. In order to obtain a clear picture of the self-concept and how it changes, let us take each of the four propositions listed above and see where and under what conditions they hold.

1. *The self-concept is based on the perceived responses of others.* We do not mean to suggest that, every time the individual notices someone responding to him in some fashion that is not consistent with his conception, he is immediately going to bring his self-concept into line with this new bit of evidence. Remember that our graduate student resisted quite a deluge of responses that she perceived as indicative of her attractiveness before she changed her conception of herself. So we might introduce a corollary to our proposition: *The more frequently the individual perceives responses that are inconsistent with his self-concept the more likely he is to change his conception of himself* (all other factors being equal).

All changes cannot be explained in terms of frequency alone. The evaluations that you get from a friend may be more influential in changing your self-concept than those you get from a dozen strangers. Or the evaluation of your professor may be given more weight than the evaluation of fellow students. Here we could say that *the more important the source of the evaluation as perceived by the individual the more likely he is to bring his self-concept in line with the evaluation* (other factors being equal). This notion of perceived "importance" of the other is not as precise a concept as we would like. Some have referred to it as the "significant other," that person or persons whom the individual considers significant enough to affect his conception of himself. Some insight can be gained by taking a closer look at the two examples we used. Why would a friend be more influential than a stranger? Obviously, we would expect the friend to be in a better position to judge our behavior, and thus we would have to pay more attention to his evaluation. In a similar fashion, the professor may be seen as the person with the expertise; and, again, you judge his importance in terms of your perception of his ability to evaluate you.

It should be clear by now that there are many dimensions to the person's self-concept. As we have said earlier, the individual thinks of himself both in terms of attributes such as intelligence, physical attractiveness, selfishness, cooperativeness, and the like, and in terms of the roles in which he sees himself. These various dimensions, although all incorporated into an organized whole that he feels is himself, may have their origin in quite diverse sources. For example, his evaluation of his intellectual ability may be derived from his perception of the evaluations of his teachers and professors; on the other hand, his evaluation of his physical attractiveness may be a result of his understanding of the ways his peers see him in that dimension—his teachers' evaluations being quite irrelevant.

As the individual goes through life, he is continually moving into new roles and his first evaluations can prove very important in establishing how he will perform throughout his tenure in those positions. This is true for a number of reasons. Those first evaluations will be all that he has to go on for some time and with the lack of conflicting evidence they are likely to be incorporated into his self-image. Once they are there, the process of perception will have the tendency to reinforce the original judgment. Remember that the individual is likely to perceive what he expects to perceive. If he thinks of himself as ambitious, then he will be more sensitive to the evaluations of others that might reinforce this perception. That is, of all the stimuli that he might select as being indicative of his ambition, he will tend to see those that are consistent with his original self-image and disregard those that are not.

In a similar fashion, the original self-evaluation will have an effect on the individual's behavior, which, following the model in Figure 4, may well be perceived by others, reacted to, and again perceived by the individual. That is, if he thinks of himself as ambitious, he will act ambitious, and will be seen and reacted to by others as ambitious. With these new reactions of others telling him he is seen as ambitious his original self-concept will be reinforced.

There is just one more factor that might be added to this

discussion. A person tends to select as his friends and associates persons who see him as he sees himself, because he feels more comfortable under these circumstances. He may avoid situations that would require a reevaluation of his self-concept. All these factors support the corollary that *the very first evaluations on a particular dimension of the self are likely to be more important than later evaluation in determining the individual's conception of himself.*

2. *The individual's conception of himself functions to direct his behavior.* To understand the functioning of this process we need to go back to the earlier discussion of role-taking ability. Remember how the individual is required to get outside himself and look back at himself. Of course, the image he has of himself will be very important in determining what goes on in his mind during this process. The final action that he decides upon will be influenced considerably by the conception he has of himself. What we are saying here is simply that when the individual asks himself, "How shall I act?" one of the important factors he considers is this conception of himself.

As in the other propositions under consideration in this section, this proposition does not hold in any absolute fashion. There are times when the individual will find that the expectations others have for him may run counter to his self-concept, and he may find it easier to conform to those expectations than to his self-image.

There are other times when it is impossible for him to act according to his self-image. Some dimensions of the self might be described as self-fulfilling. Most persons can act ambitious if they feel that they are ambitious, or can act lazy if they feel that they are lazy. However, this does not hold for all dimensions. You may come to think of yourself as a potential track star, running the 100-yard dash in 9.2 seconds. However, it takes more than a conception of yourself to enable you to behave (run) in this fashion. It is, therefore, meaningful to talk about persons as having realistic or unrealistic conceptions of themselves. Parents, allowing their emotions to govern their judgment, often lead their children to think of themselves in unrealistically ambitious terms: "Johnnie, you're going to be the best student in your class." Then Johnnie goes to school and finds that he cannot perform in accordance with the conception that he has developed of himself. Downward re-evaluations of one's self-concept can be painful. Again, the importance of early peer relations, which we mentioned earlier, is evidence of a need to counter the unrealistic evaluation of parents.

3. *The individual's perceptions of others' responses are a fairly accurate reflection of the actual responses that the others are directing toward him.* To put this another way, we are saying that most people are pretty good role-takers. That is, they learn to accurately perceive the ways others are responding to them. It is not necessary to elaborate here, since we have discussed this under the headings of perception and role-taking ability. We can summarize by saying that anything that stands in the way of accurate perception or good role-taking would tend to diminish the validity of this proposition.

4. *The actual responses of others are based on evaluative responses to the individual's behavior.* Remember that we defined behavior to include both action and appearance. All we are implying is that in the interactive setting the other's action and behavior can, at least in part, be seen as evaluative feedback.

This brings us to one further consideration, which is of central importance in our analysis. That is, who is the "other"? Under the discussion of influences on self-concept change, when we talked about the importance that the individual places on the other we mentioned the "significant other," as that other whose importance or expertness is seen as great enough to influence the individual's conception of himself. However, as we have implied, there is not just one "other"; there are many. In a later chapter, we will talk about *reference groups* as those groups the individual uses as a source of self-evaluation. Mead described this when he used the concept of the *generalized other*. He said that it was only when the individual could get outside himself and assume the role of the *group as a whole* that he would establish a stable conception of himself. By the generalized other is meant the internal way in which the individual puts together the responses of others, weighing some highly, ignoring some, and so on, and finally comes up with a general evaluation of their responses. When an instructor says to a colleague, "My class was bored with my lecture today," he is reflecting his image of the generalized other's response to him. He did not take one person's response alone, nor did he take a poll and ask each person to indicate if he was bored so that he could add up all the responses and find a proportion. What he did was to take a response here (someone yawns), more there (three students are reading newspapers), and a few more over there (the back row is asleep), and put these together to get an impression of the group as a whole. This is the generalized other. It does not exist in reality, only in the head of the person under consideration.

Other Issues Regarding the Self-concept

In the last section, we emphasized the importance of the evaluations of others in establishing the individual's conception of himself. This emphasis is not meant to exclude the possibility of other sources of evidence about the self. For example, Leon Festinger[6] suggests that one important contribution to the understanding of the self-concept comes from the individual's comparison of his perception of his own behavior with what he sees in the behavior of others. If you are uncertain whether to consider yourself "radical," or "kind," or "selfish," or whatever, you may depend upon your comparison of yourself with others.

So we see that there are at least two ways of learning about

[6] Leon A. Festinger, "A Theory of Social Comparison," *Human Relations*, vol. 7, pp. 117–140, 1954.

oneself—from one's perceptions of the responses of other persons to his behavior and from the comparison of one's behavior with the behavior of others. The two approaches should be seen as complementary, since one does not exclude the other.

The study of the self-concept brings up a number of other interesting issues that we can touch on only briefly here. One popular concern is with man's search for *identity*. The importance of knowing yourself has been the topic of many an essay. Psychologists tell us that a consistent concept of self is essential for mental well-being. We have seen earlier in this chapter how a person's self-concept will affect the individual's behavior.

This brings us to another issue. Is the self-concept simply a social construct or is there a "true self" ready to be actualized? Is a person ambitious because others have told him he was ambitious and thus led him to come to see himself that way, or is there something about his nature that intrinsically makes him ambitious and social encounters only bring this to his attention? In answer to this intriguing question, we take the position that there are undoubtedly some dimensions of the self that are more than just the reflections of the evaluations of or comparisons with others. These may take the form of artistic talents or physiological attributes. However, we must emphasize the importance of social influences even in these areas. Our example of the graduate students demonstrated the importance of social definitions even in the area of physical attractiveness. If this is true in areas that have clear biological or physical sources, how much more must it be true in those areas where there is no connection.

There is a final issue that often comes up when the self-concept is discussed. Does the individual have one general self-concept or does he have a separate self-concept for each social setting? This can be answered best after we have covered a later section on groups. For now, we can say that to think exclusively of a single self-concept is misleading. Although it is true that when an individual moves into a new group he brings with him a conception of himself based on earlier encounters and some dimensions of the old self are reenforced, at the same time many dimensions of the self may not be relevant in the new setting. As you move from your work, to school, to a date, the image you have of yourself naturally changes because the same type of expectations do not carry over to the new settings.

THE INTERACTIONAL SETTING

In some of the following chapters, we will discuss the group and its importance in accounting for the influence that society has on the individual. In this section, we need only mention that the interactional situation is a group situation and will vary in its effect in the many ways that the group can vary. For example, in some rigidly formal groups like the military, all the expectations are clearly spelled out and conformity is demanded. Other settings such as a long-established street gang may be very structured in the sense that the expectations have been well defined over years of interactional exchange but still the interaction remains completely informal, with no explicit mention of the standards of expectations. Whether the situation is structured or unstructured, formal or informal, personal or impersonal, will affect the notions of communication, perception, role-taking, and self-concept development that we have discussed here. As these questions are dealt with in later chapters, the student should increase his understanding of how the group affects the individual along these lines.

SUMMARY

At least part of the process that goes on in our minds as we are thinking consists of coming up with alternative possible actions. On the basis of this consideration of alternatives, the individual chooses the behavior that seems appropriate for him. When is he confronted with another individual or a group, he must put himself in the place of the other and be able to anticipate how that other would respond to the behavior he is considering. This is called role-taking. Persons vary in their ability to take roles with respect to their familiarity with the other or others involved, their familiarity with the social situation, the feedback that is available to them, and their general role-taking ability that they bring into the situation.

Out of this interaction with others, the individual develops a conception of what he is like. This organization of qualities that the individual attributes to himself results from his perception of the ways others see or respond to him. Once his self-concept is formed, he uses it to help determine his own behavior. The formation of the self is a group process and will be understood more clearly after the discussion of the group which follows.

SUGGESTED REFERENCES

* Cooley, Charles H.: *Human Nature and the Social Order* (1st ed., 1902), Schocken Books, Inc., New York, 1964.
  The classic work of Cooley in which he presents his ideas on the primary group and the looking-glass self.

Dewey, John: *Human Nature and Conduct*, Holt, Rinehart & Winston, Inc., New York, 1922.
  Dewey's classic treatise on the place of impulse, habit, and reflective thinking in the organization of human behavior.

Faris, Robert E. L.: *Social Psychology*, The Ronald Press Company, New York, 1952.
  Excellent discussion of the emergence of consciousness and the self in the tradition of George Herbert Mead.

* Gergen, Kenneth J.: *The Concept of Self*, Holt, Rinehart & Winston, Inc., New York, 1971.
  Presentation of a variety of ideas relating to many dimensions of the self with special emphasis on correlates of self-esteem.

* Goffman, Erving: *Presentation of Self in Everyday Life*, Doubleday & Company, Inc., Garden City, N.Y., 1959 (Anchor Books).
  The most readable and insightful book into how people present themselves to each other in everyday life.

* _____: *Interaction Ritual*, Doubleday & Company, Inc., Garden City, N.Y., 1967 (Anchor Books).
  Expansion of Goffman's ideas on face-to-face behavior. Deals with the nature the self must have if its possessor is to receive the type of responses he wishes.

Gordon, Chad, and Kenneth J. Gergen (eds.): *The Self in Social Interaction*, John Wiley & Sons, Inc., New York, 1968.
  Both classic and contemporary articles and essays on the self.

* Hamackek, Don E.: *Encounters with the Self*, Holt, Rinehart & Winston, Inc., New York, 1971.
  Clear presentation of the development of the self and its func-

tion in interpersonal encounters. This book is designed to help
the reader in developing his self-concept.

* Klapp, Orrin E.: *Collective Search for Identity*, Holt, Rinehart &
Winston, Inc., New York, 1969.
Deals with fads, fashions, heroes, celebrities, recreations, and
the like, from the point of view of what they tell about the
identity search in a mass society.

McCall, George J., and J. L. Simmons: *Identities and Interactions:
An Examination of Human Associations in Everyday Life,* The
Free Press, New York, 1966.
A clear and interesting exploration of what happens when
ordinary persons come together in familiar settings.

* Stein, Maurice, Arthur J. Vidich, and David M. White: *Identity
and Anxiety,* The Free Press, New York, 1960.
A collection of essays on the problems of identity in a complex
society.

* Strauss, Anselm: *The Social Psychology of George Herbert
Mead,* The University of Chicago Press, Chicago, 1956.
A collection of the essays of Mead, including his classic "Mind,
Self and Society."

_____: *Mirrors and Masks: The Search for Identity*, The Free
Press, New York, 1959.
An expansion on Mead's ideas on the self and how it evolves in
social interaction.

* Sullivan, Harry Stack: *The Interpersonal Theory of Psychiatry,*
W. W. Norton & Company, Inc., New York, 1953.
Presents the ideas of one of the great leaders in the field of
psychiatry. Valuable as a treatment of both socialization and
the emergent self.

* References marked with asterisk are available in paperback.

SIX

VARIATIONS IN THE HUMAN GROUP

Groups can be classified in an almost infinite number of ways. Social psychologists have chosen certain ways that seem valuable in helping them to explain human social behavior. There is little question that the concept of groups is an important part of social psychology. In this chapter, we will deal with some of the ways groups differ. In the chapter that follows our concern will be directed toward commonalities—characteristics that are true of all groups.

THE GROUP DEFINED

As patterns of interpersonal relationships endure over a period of time, the individuals involved begin to see themselves as belonging together, come to expect certain reactions from the others, and realize that the others expect certain things of them. *This collection of two or more persons who interact and share common norms and whose social roles interlock* make up what we call a *social group.* Note the three conditions that define the group: *interaction, shared norms,* and *interlocking roles.*

Most social psychologists consider interaction as the central concept in delimiting the group. The group exists insofar as the individuals are responding and are being responded to, that is, interacting. Shibutani[1] emphasized the importance of this dimension by suggesting that a group be regarded as consisting of "men acting together as a unit." The emphasis is on the action, not on the collection of persons. He suggests that interest in the study of the group ought to center not so much upon membership as upon participation. One can see how conceiving of the individuals involved as participants rather than members places a different perspective on the analysis of the group. This will be brought out in this chapter and the next chapter in which we discuss group processes.

The shared norms that constitute part of every group are a result of several factors. We defined norms in an earlier chapter as those rules or standards for behavior that are shared by the members of the group or the society. At that point, we were discussing the topic of society. Here, when we are concerned more directly with the group, we must take an even closer look at this important concept and how it affects the group operation. Although we will reserve the detailed analysis for later in this chapter, it is important to point out here something about the origin of group norms.

When we say that in order for the group to exist the members or participants must share common norms, we mean that they must have sets of standards or expectations that will govern their behavior and will allow them to predict how others will behave. The group members may bring these expectations with them as they come into the group so these expectations may reflect a larger cultural milieu. Or the expectations may emerge over a period of initial interaction in which the norms are formulated on the basis of the actions and reactions of the participants.

[1] Tamotsu Shibutani, *Society and Personality*, Prentice-Hall, Inc., Englewood Cliffs, N.J., 1961, pp. 32–39.

We learned in the chapter on society how roles are a special type of norms that do not apply universally to all members of the group but rather apply to those members who occupy particular positions. The comments regarding norms apply equally to roles. What has been added in the definition of the group is that the roles must be interlocking; that is, the particular set of expectations that are directed toward an individual who occupies a particular position includes prescriptions for how he is expected to behave, not just on his own, but in *relation to the other members of the group.*

Let us put together this discussion of the meaning of the concept of group by considering an example with which every student is familiar: Does your social psychology class fit the criteria for a social group? First, is there interaction? Does the behavior on the part of some of the participants call out responses on the part of others? You probably do not run into each other or try to sit in the same chair or continue talking throughout the lecture; so it seems safe to say that there is some interaction going on. The next question: Are there shared norms? You could probably list any number. The class agrees to start at 10:10 every Monday, Wednesday, and Friday; they all meet in the same room, and so on. This example brings out the point that we have made about the origin of these norms. Although every member of the class may agree that the class should start at 10:10, this norm did not emerge as a result of the interaction of this particular group but rather was imposed upon the group because it was part of a larger social system (the college). Now, your professor may be in the habit of coming ten minutes late to class so that the lecture does not start until 10:20. After a time, the students realize this and do not bother to get there until the later time. Here, a new norm has emerged; this new one is based on the interaction of the participants, not imposed by some system of which they are a part.

The third criterion requires that the roles be interlocking.

There are two formalized positions that make up most class-room settings: the teacher and the student. The role of the teacher involves presenting material, either in a lecture or by leading discussion; examining the students; and usually providing them with some evaluation of their performance (a grade) at the end of a specified time period. The student, in his position, is expected to listen to the lectures, take notes, perform on examinations, and the like. Note how closely the roles interlock. If there were no students there could be no teacher. Without the teacher, the students would have nothing to take notes on and no one to examine them. So far, the example has dealt with the formal positions imposed from outside. Note that the roles listed are not the only roles to which the individual is expected to conform. If the class is structured so that the group interacts over time with some degree of freedom, new roles emerge that are solely the result of the interaction of that particular group. One person may emerge as the discussion leader, always ready to make significant contributions to group discussions. After a while, this person will be looked to by both the students and the teacher to perform this role when the class session is open for discussion. Note the difference between the role of the instructor, which is defined by the institutional aspects of the setting, and the role of the discussion leader, which emerged as a result of the social interaction.

AGGREGATES AND CATEGORIES

Certain phenomena to which the word "group" is frequently attached do not fit our definition, and we shall exclude them from our present consideration of groups. The first is the situation in which we find a number of individuals together in geographical proximity but with little, if any, organization or interaction. A crowd waiting for a street car or the spectators at a baseball game would be examples of this. We shall use the word "aggregate" for this phenomenon and shall deal with it in some detail in a later chapter when we consider crowd behavior.

The other phenomenon that does not fit our definition of group we shall call a category, or class. Here we are referring to any plural number of individuals who can be responded to or classified by a single individual characteristic. All high school graduates, all males, all student body presidents, all homeowners, and all taxpayers are examples of categories. Note that the individuals who make up a class or category are likely to be geographically dispersed and not in a position to interact with one another. Both of these concepts have an important place in social psychology and will be dealt with from time to time through the text, but they must not be confused with the concept of group, which is the immediate concern of this chapter.

Any close investigation of the concept of the group as we have presented it here should lead the student to the realization that the group can take a large number of forms. It is most obvious that groups vary in size. Equally obvious is the fact that they vary in the types of activities engaged in. In addition, they provide quite differing types of relationships and are not at all alike in the influence or effect they have on the individuals involved. In the section that follows we shall consider some of the ways of looking at the variations that exist in groups.

THE INTENSITY OF RELATIONSHIPS—PRIMARY AND SECONDARY

One of the major contributions of sociology to the area we call social psychology is the concept of the primary group. It was first introduced in 1925 by Charles Cooley,[2] and it re-

[2] Charles H. Cooley, *Social Organization* (1st ed., 1909), Schocken Books, Inc., New York, 1962, pp. 23–31.

mains one of the most valuable concepts in the study of groups. Let us consider Cooley's own words:

> By primary groups I mean those characterized by intimate face-to-face association and cooperation. They are primary in several senses, but chiefly in that they are fundamental in forming the social nature and ideals of the individual. . . . Primary groups are primary in the sense that they give the individual his earliest and completest experience of social unity, and also in the sense that they do not change in the same degree as more elaborate relations, but form a comparatively permanent source out of which the latter are ever springing.

Much has been written about the primary group since Cooley's ideas were published. The notion of reference groups, to be discussed in the next section, was seen by some as a substitute for the primary group concept; however, certain dimensions of the primary group concept sustain its importance to social psychology.

Cooley emphasized the importance of the primary group in the socialization of the child. He mentioned the family and neighborhood peer groups among the most important primary groups for each person. Although it would be hard to disagree with this contention, it may be somewhat misleading in that it does not give appropriate attention to the role of the primary group in adult life. If it is to be a useful concept in social psychology, we must answer the question: What underlies the primary relationship that makes it different from other relationships? Various authors have listed a number of features—informality of members, smallness in size, high solidarity, mutual acceptance, intimate knowledge of each other, spontaneity of behavior, long duration, frequency of interaction, and homogeneity of membership have all been considered as important features. What seems to be important is that the primary group provides an atmosphere in which the individuals involved can exchange intimate knowledge about each other, can act and react with some degree of spontaneity, and can thereby provide the individuals with a realistic conception of themselves and a view of what others expect of them. However, in order to accomplish this end, the group must be such that the individual will not just learn these expectations, but will take them to heart—internalize them and make them part of his value system. Therefore, apparently the group must be small and informal, it must have a high degree of solidarity and mutual acceptance, and it must exist over a long enough period of time and with enough frequency of interaction among its members for these conditions to be maintained. Certainly there may be situations in which all these conditions are not present and still the basic features for the primary group are met. A love affair need not exist very long before it develops clearly into a full-fledged primary relationship, with all the important dimensions, but without a long duration.

The important factor in understanding the primary group is the quality of the relationships that exist among the members of the group. The members have a unique emotional attachment to one another that does not exist in other types of groups. Their concern for the other members goes beyond the immediate situation.

The Family as a Primary Group

In our society, it is indisputably true that the family is the most primary group for most if not all individuals. It is the first group that the individual is confronted with, and it is intimately involved in the formative stages of his development. His conception of himself and his introduction to the norms and expectations of society are begun through the family. For this reason, we shall have more to say about the family when we discuss socialization in a later chapter. Here it is valuable to show some of the features that make the family different from other primary groups.

Perhaps the major feature that differentiates the family from other primary groups is that it is not only a group, but also an institution. What are the consequences of this? Remember, an institution consists of those norms, roles, and values that society develops around certain of its basic needs that are lasting and that reflect some central values of the society. Therefore, most of the norms that govern behavior within the family are not a result of interaction among the specific individuals involved but rather are norms that have been passed on to them from previous generations. The father is expected to have the responsibility for maintaining the level of monetary resources. In other words, he goes out and works and brings home the money. The wife-mother may or may not work, but it remains her responsibility to see to it that the children are cared for. Although these norms change from time to time, they have persisted for many generations within our society without widespread deviation. Anthropologists tell us that other cultures may use quite different sets of norms to fulfill the functions of the family, so it cannot be the functions themselves that establish the norms but rather they are set by the custom or norm of the particular society we live in.

We might characterize the social organization of the family as having a rigid *division of labor*. The three positions—father-husband, mother-wife, and child—that make up the nuclear family in our society have roles that clearly differentiate them from one another. This is important because it contrasts the family with other primary groups, which are likely to have an undifferentiated membership in which the norms and roles emerge out of the interaction of the actual membership.

Friendship or Peer Group

We usually think of the peer group as made up of persons with similar interests and characteristics. In adolescence, the peer group is usually make up of persons of the same age and sex. In adult life, the groups may be more heterogeneous but still very similar in background. Membership in the peer group is voluntary, and the activities engaged in are usually a result of consensus that develops out of group interaction. It may take the form of a group of neighborhood women who get together every morning after husbands have gone to work and the children are off to school. During their kaffeklatsch, they discuss the problems that confront them in the other roles that society demands of them. In this primary group, the membership may be relatively undifferentiated; however, this does not mean that there is no differentiation at all. One woman may be seen as the instigator, who can be relied upon to give suggestions for activities that the group might engage in. Another might be the storyteller who will be looked to by the others to entertain them through coffee with her clever stories. However, in contrast with the family this division of labor is minimal. The norms in this type of group are likely to be less explicit than they are in other groups in the sense that they are not likely to be spelled out in a verbal fashion. However, this should not be taken as a sign of their absence or even as an indicator of their weakness. For example, in some groups such as the one we have discussed, confidentiality may be a most important norm. Those groups of women that chose this norm agree that what is said over coffee is to go no further. This is a very functional norm for a friendship group, for it then frees the individuals to confide on an intimate level and thus maintain the primary relationship. Violation of the norm of confidentiality in this type of group cannot be tolerated. Discovery that the secrets shared over coffee were disclosed to an outsider is likely to result in one of the most severe punishments that the group can inflict on its members—expulsion.

Let us now systematically consider the differences between the two primary groups that we have discussed—the family and peer group. First, one is governed to a large extent by rules imposed by the larger society, whereas the other develops most of its norms from the interaction of the group. Second, the family shows a high degree of differentiation or division of labor, whereas the peer group is much less differentiated. Third, the family is a relatively involuntary group that some members (the children) have no choice about entering and that none of the members can leave with ease. The peer group is much more voluntary: members can come and go with considerably more freedom than in the family. As an important note about our remarks regarding the voluntary leaving of a primary group: One might be misled by these remarks into thinking that one can come and go with the least consideration for the consequence of this action. However, remember that one of the characteristics of the primary group is that it provides the type of atmosphere in which one can disclose intimate information regarding oneself. Considering then that the other members of the primary group know a great deal about the person that is not public knowledge, he might well think twice before he alienates the other members of the group by leaving them.

After contrasting these two types of groups, we should again ask what they have in common that allows us to classify both as primary groups. Note that both groups are intimate, face-to-face groups, in which there is a high degree of solidarity, spontaneity, and mutual acceptance. The group members share intimate knowledge about each other and have a unique emotional relationship with one another.

Why do people join and place such importance on these groups that we have called primary? What are the goals of these groups? Some authors have suggested that the group is an end in itself. Without disputing the need for primary types of relationships, it seems more plausible to talk about the goals of the group as being friendship, love, recognition, and emotional security. These values are important to the well-being of the individual and are not obtainable through the secondary types of relationships.

Secondary Groups

Cooley never discussed secondary groups, and the concept is probably not nearly so important as the primary-group concept. When we talk about secondary groups or relationships, we are concerned with the types of relationship that are held together primarily, if not solely, because of the necessity of cooperation that exists for the fulfillment of the aims of the group or the goals of the individual participants. In the primary group, individuals conform to the norms because they feel it is right to do so or because they have an emotional commitment to the other members of the group; in the secondary group, persons conform to the norms because it is *practical* or in their interest to do so. In the secondary group, the norms are almost always set down by some larger, more formal, system of relationships; and the actual interaction among members is frequently of short duration with little involvement on a personal level. When you go to your bank to make a deposit, chances are that your relationship with the teller is on a secondary level. Your major concern in regard to this other person is in terms of one role that he is to perform in his position as teller. You are not concerned with his children, how his stomach feels, or what he will be doing tomorrow. You are concerned only with the practical question of whether he will deposit your money without error. During the day, you may enter into a large number of secondary relationships—a gas station attendant, a professor, a customer in the store where you work, and so on. In each instance, the relationship is primarily concerned with getting a job done—cashing a check, filling a gas tank, exchanging information, or selling a car. After this is accomplished, you go your separate ways with little concern for the other until the same need again arises.

However, it should be clear from careful consideration of these examples that not all secondary-group relationships remain secondary. There is probably a degree of primary relationship in all of them. If you have been going to the same bank for several years, you may know your teller by name and may even know a few things about his life. This leads us to suggest that it may make more sense to talk about primary and secondary *relationships* rather than primary and secondary *groups per se.* The careful reader will have already noted that frequently in the discussion in this section we used the word "relationship" rather than "group." It should be clear now that some of the interaction that goes on in the family is more on a secondary than on a primary level (when a husband and wife sit down to figure out the family budget, their relationship may be more secondary than primary). We might say that a primary group is one in which most of the relationships or exchanges are primary and that a secondary group is one in which most of the exchanges are secondary relationships.

From this point of view, we might conclude that most of what we have said in this section has been about relationships, not groups. Few groups fit the extremes of being completely primary or completely secondary.

REFERENCE GROUPS

Compared with the notion of the primary group, the concept of the reference group is relatively new. Social psychologists do not agree completely as to what they mean by the concept; however, there is general agreement that the *concept of reference group* is most useful when it is used to refer to *that group, real or imaginary, whose standpoint is being used as the frame of reference of the individual.* In other words, it is the group that the individual uses to establish his perspective in the organization of his perceptions of the world—whether that world be concerned with how he sees others, the group, or even himself. Let us consider what is implied in such a definition.

The reference-group concept is meaningful only when seen from the perspective of the individual. In order to identify a reference group, we must look to the individual and ask which group or groups he is using as a frame of reference in determining his perceptual world. The individual need not be a member of this group. As a matter of fact, he frequently uses as reference groups those groups to whose membership he aspires as well as those of which he is already a member. Recruits use the established soldier as their frame of reference in determining their judgment as to how they are to act in military situations. They compare their own performance with their reference group as a means of self-evaluation. The rookie looks to the veteran, the freshman to the senior. In each of these instances, the prospective member of a group has selected as models the established members of the group and uses them to furnish him with perspectives for seeing the world.

Over a period of time an individual will use a large number of reference groups. Almost every new situation requires a new reference group. In some instances, the reference group may not even exist but may be an imaginary group that the individual has constructed out of his various experiences. However, this discussion should not lead to the conclusion that membership groups are not reference groups. It seems to be true that the degree to which the individual's membership group serves as a reference group is dependent upon the individual's satisfaction or dissatisfaction with the group. It seems fair to say that primary groups are always reference groups, because the type of relationship demands that the individual take the perspective of the group members in order to meaningfully interact with them.

Remembering our discussion of the formation of the self-concept, we can see the significance of the reference group for the individual. In the analysis of the self we said that the individual must get outside himself and look back at himself as an object from the perspective of the other. Later in our discussion, we pointed out how the "other" was frequently a group and that the individual generalized those responses of others into what we called the generalized other. Now we can see that the generalized other is the individual's reference group because the individual uses the perspectives of this group in determining his conception of himself.

Some of the studies of reference groups show the diverse ways in which the individual can be affected by his choice of reference groups. One study of soldiers' morale attitudes found that there was very little difference in morale between overseas noncombatants and the men stationed in the United States. The results were accounted for by considering the groups that the soldiers were using as perspectives in evaluating their situations. Those noncombat soldiers overseas were more likely to use as their reference group the combat soldiers, whereas the soldiers still at home used their civilian friends for comparison. Being overseas is bad, but compared with fighting, things could be worse. Being in the United States was good service, but compared with being out of the Army it was pretty restrictive.[3]

The use of the concept of reference group has frequently violated our definition of a group. A category, which describes an individual characteristic, does not make up a group. "Democrats," "Catholics," and "middle class" are terms that describe classes of persons, not groups. The category is not defined by interaction between members. However, it may be helpful to note that researchers dealing with the study of society's effects on the individual have referred to such categories as reference groups. They are saying that the individual can use these categories as perspective for his evaluation of certain aspects of his perceptual world. One study showed that reminding students that they were Roman Catholics tended to make them use the Catholic church as a reference group in viewing religious and ethical matters. These subjects gave

[3] Robert K. Merton and A. S. Kitt, "Contributions to the Theory of Reference Group Behavior," in G. E. Swanson, T. M. Newcomb, and E. L. Hartley (eds.), Readings in Social Psychology, Holt, Rinehart & Winston, Inc., New York, 1952.

responses to attitude questionnaires quite different from those of another group of Catholic students who had not been reminded of the religious affiliation.[4] This tells us that the individual can use a wide variety of "groups" as frames of reference for determining his values, norms, and perceptions of the world. It points out the importance of knowing the reference group that an individual is using at a particular moment in order to understand that person's behavior.

GROUP SIZE

The size of the group has some obvious consequence for the behavior of the members. The definition of the group does not restrict its size. It could range from two to thousands or more. But the difference between a group made up of two persons and one made up of five can immediately be seen. When the group gets even larger, more changes are evident. It is therefore important that we look at the effects of the size of the group on the interaction of the members.

Small Groups

In the past twenty years, the study of small groups has become very popular in social psychology. Much of this emphasis developed after the discovery that groups could be taken into research laboratories, where researchers could conduct highly controlled experiments. This led to a controversy: Could findings derived from artificially contrived groups constructed for experimental purpose be used to make generalizations about "natural" groups? The controversy goes on; however, much of the laboratory research on small groups

[4] W. W. Charters and Theodore M. Newcomb, "Some Attitudinal Effects of Experimentally Increased Salience of a Membership Group," in E. E. Maccoby, T. M. Newcomb, and E. L. Hartley (eds.), *Readings in Social Psychology*, 3d ed., Holt, Rinehart & Winston, Inc., New York, 1958, p. 276.

has been fruitful in producing generalizations that are testable in more natural settings, although some of the research has been so contrived and artificial as to be worthless for that purpose. This popularity of small-group research has called to the attention of every social psychologist the importance of the small group in accounting for the dynamics of the relationship between man and society.

The first question that usually comes up when dealing with this topic is: How small must a group be to be a small group? Most authorities have long since given up trying to provide a numerical answer to this question. It does not make sense to say that if the group numbers twelve it is small, but if it numbers thirteen it is large. What seems more feasible is to suggest that it is the potential consequence of the size of the group that determines where it is small or not. One criterion might be: If the size of the group is such that every member can potentially have firsthand face-to-face interaction with all the other members, then it is a small group. Or one might approach it from the other direction and suggest that a group is no longer small when there is a tendency for the members to slip into subgroups during periods of free interaction. None of these criteria are completely satisfactory in themselves, but a careful consideration of them gives the student an accurate picture of the concept we are referring to when we use the term "small group." It is almost always used to refer to groups that are small enough not to be splintered into subgroups and where complete and inclusive interaction is possible.

It may be more fruitful to start at the small end of the scale in considering small groups. We shall reject the notion that the individual can be conceived of as a group of one and move to the question: Do two persons interacting make a group? This certainly falls within our more formal definition of a group, but it can be seen immediately that this is a unique type of group, different from groups of any other size. In the two-person group, or *dyad* as it is sometimes called, the interaction is uncomplicated with the need to take into consideration any group members other than the two in the interacting setting. In our presentation of the communication model and our initial discussion of role-taking we dealt almost exclusively with the two-person group because of the ease in analysis. However, communication and role-taking efficiency are not the only factors that can be considered in studying the dyad. For example, we have said nothing about the quality of the relationship that exists between the two persons. What are the sentiments or attitudes they hold toward each other? Does their liking or disliking of each other affect their perception, communication, or role-taking?

Although we cannot review the whole of the literature on attitudes, some of the work done on dyads exemplifies how this subject might be approached. For example, the work of Heider[5] and Newcomb[6] on what is termed *balance theory* makes the point that the attitudes of individuals toward each other affect their attitudes toward nonperson objects in their environment. In the most simplistic of terms, these researchers are saying that if you like the person you are with and that person has a strong positive attitude toward some object that confronts both of you and you feel negative about that object, then you both will feel uncomfortable (in the language of the theory: The situation is unbalanced). In addition, they claim that persons prefer balanced settings and that, therefore, there will be a tendency to try to bring the situation into balance— to reduce the tension or feeling of discomfort. Imagine that you and your friend are faced with a vote on a school bond issue about which you disagree. In the simple situation described here, the situation may be brought into balance in three different ways. First, you can change your attitude toward the object—"If my good friend Joe feels so strongly,

[5] F. Heider, *The Psychology of Interpersonal Relations*, John Wiley & Sons, Inc., New York, 1958.
[6] Theodore M. Newcomb, "Interpersonal Balance," in R. P. Abelson *et al.* (eds.), *Theories of Cognitive Consistency: A Sourcebook*, Rand McNally & Co., Chicago, 1968.

maybe I'd better take a new look at the issue." Second, you might try to get your friend to change his attitude and vote with you against the bond. Either of these changes would bring the situation to the point where two persons who like each other share a common feeling about the object with which they are confronted—a balanced situation. There is a third possibility: If you cannot change your position or get your friend to change his, there may be a tendency for you to change your attitude regarding your friend—"Well, if you won't vote against the school bond, to hell with you." Two persons who dislike each other and hold contrasting views exemplify another balanced situation. Although of necessity our presentation of balance theory oversimplifies the ideas and runs the risk of being misleading, the perceptive student should be able to see how the extension of a model like this could be very useful in gaining an understanding of the ways the interpersonal attitudes affect the behavior of individuals and their attitudes toward other persons and nonperson objects.

This leads us to a consideration of the three-person group, or *triad*. What does it do to a two-person group when we add a third member? This adds a number of interesting complications. The balance theorists are quick to point out that the triad is generally less stable than the dyad, with much more potential of being out of balance. In some of the earliest writings on small groups, the sociologist Georg Simmel[7] claimed that there was a tendency for triads to divide into a dyad and an isolate, and, as a result, the isolate could gain by forming a coalition with one of the members of the dyad. Take as an example a husband and wife who are interacting with her mother. There might be a tendency for the spouses to form a dyad and leave the mother as an isolate. This, then, puts the latter in a position where she can side with one or the other, form a coalition, and gain power to control the situa-

[7] Georg Simmel, *The Sociology of Georg Simmel* (Kurt Wolff trans., ed., and intro.), The Free Press, New York, 1950.

tion. Perhaps an even better example is the child, who by siding with one parent or the other finds he can control the family situation.

This type of example is valuable in explaining another type of analysis that might be used in the study of triads. Goffman,[8] in his study of the way persons present themselves in everyday life, suggests that it is possible to conceive of persons as putting on performances for those about them. In the example used above, he might say that the husband and the wife are putting on a performance for the mother. The understanding of their individual actions is a function of the *awareness* of the persons involved. If we take the behavior of the wife, as an example, how do we account for the fact that she is cheerful and talkative when the mother enters and creates the triad. Now the husband (in Goffman's theatrical terms) has been backstage with his wife. That is, he was with his wife in the moments before the mother entered. He knows that they were having a violent disagreement and that his wife was on the verge of tears. Because he had this awareness, he understands the meaning of her performance and may join her in the show, which is designed to make the audience (the mother) think that they are a happily married couple. However, he may want to be careful in his performance that he does not let his fellow actor get the upper hand and win the sympathy of the audience at his expense. He does not want the mother and daughter to form a coalition against him. He knows that the two of them have been backstage together (in his wife's childhood) and that the mother may be engaging in a performance with her daughter with him as the audience. (That is, the mother, having had similar experiences with her daughter, knows that the talkativeness is a way of hiding tears, sees this as her daughter's way of telling her how sad she is, and plays along so that the husband will not know of her awareness.) This

[8] Erving Goffman, *Presentation of Self in Everyday Life*, Doubleday & Company, Inc., Garden City, N.Y., 1959.

example is presented here to demonstrate the importance of *awareness* in the interpersonal situation and to show how complex the analysis of a group of only three persons can become.

If we are to follow our sequence on to a four-person group we simply add more complexity. An important factor emerges as the size of our group moves beyond three. The complexity is not just in the analysis that the social psychologist might be making. The situation becomes complex to the individuals involved. Consequently, the group participants tend to ease the complexity by responding to others in generalized fashion rather than as to a collection of other individuals. There is an increasing tendency for the individual to respond to the group as a whole, to look for attitudes and responses of the generalized other, not individual others. By perceiving the group as more than the sum of the individual members, the social psychologist as well as the participant can respond meaningfully to the small group.

The analysis of small groups of varying sizes is of central importance in social psychology and has been or will be discussed in detail in other parts of the book. The analysis of primary groups presented earlier in this chapter deals with groups of this size. In the next chapter, we shall be dealing with various structural aspects of groups, and the discussion will be on the importance of understanding the norms of the group and the role differentiation that emerges from the interaction of group members. Later chapters will be concerned with the functioning of the group and the process involved in socialization of new members, decision making, and other group processes. All this is relevant to the understanding of the small group.

Large Groups

When the group goes beyond the size that would qualify it as a small group—when it begins to fragment, when face-to-face interaction is restricted—several things begin to happen to its structure. Perhaps most obvious is the tendency for the group to become more formal—that is, explicit attention is given to the norms of the group. At first it may be a matter of the rules being verbalized, whereas in the smaller group they could just be assumed or implied from the interaction patterns of the members. With verbalization, the rules of the group become more formal, since there is less leeway for individual interpretation and the ease with which they can be changed is reduced. As the group gets even larger, it may become necessary for the norms to be put in written form. This reduces even more the flexibility of the group.

We are careful not to tie this analysis to any specific number because some groups of a rather large size can be run without formal rules and regulations and some relatively small groups operate according to rigidly formal rules. A street-corner gang might have fifty active members, who operate together efficiently without any explicit mention of the expectations that govern their behavior, but a commission with five members or a board of directors with eight members may operate within the strictest set of formal regulations.

There has been a tendency in social psychology to lose interest in the group when it gets too big and formal. As a matter of fact, the word "group" is frequently dropped in favor of the term "formal organization," and the analysis is left for the sociologists. Perhaps the division of labor between sociologists and social psychologists is for the best, and perhaps we should leave to sociologists the specific analyses of the structure and functioning of the complex social organizations of society. However, in modern society the individual is so enmeshed in systems of bureaucracies that social psychologists should not overlook the influence of these systems on the individual. Much has been written on the consequences to a society that becomes so bureaucratized that the person completely loses any individual identity and is seen only in terms of the position he holds within the bureaucracy. He is a number, and the fact that behind that number is a person who has feelings, needs, and emotions is of little concern to a society whose major concern is with the efficient operation of the bureaucratic machine. Just how far in this direction have we gone in this society and what are the consequences for the members of society? It is not possible for us to answer a question of this magnitude in the space available here. We can only look at some of the conditions that do exist and speculate about their possible consequences.

Anyone who visits the business or financial district of a large city will be struck with the uniformity in the dress of the businessmen there. The gray flannel suit of the "organization man" has long been used to demonstrate how the bureaucracy stifles any form of creativity. Picture the corporation employee who gets up in the morning in his suburban tract home, which has exactly the same floor plan as all the homes within two miles of his house. His wife drives him to the commuter train in a General Motors car that looks just like the neighbors' cars, all of which are now on their way to the train station. He joins his fellow businessmen, all wearing gray flannel suits, all carrying the local paper, all getting on the train and opening their paper to the stock report. In the city from eight till five, he engages in very specialized duties for the corporation that employs him, and at five-thirty he is back on the train, now reading the *Wall Street Journal*. At home he and all his neighbors in their separate homes sit down, have a martini, and watch the evening news. After dinner, he says goodnight to the two children, thinks to himself what a coincidence that all of his friends at work also have two children, and then goes back to television.

This is an extreme example, but by no means fictional. Many people in our country do live like the man described above. Uniformity makes for efficiency whether it be in building homes or selecting ties. What is the consequence of a life filled with uniformity? Does it really stifle creativity? Insofar as we can say that creativity is the product of diverse experiences, we can certainly conclude that it does. The businessman in his mold has a very limited range of experiences to draw upon. However, insofar as creativity requires a mind free from mundane tasks, you could well argue in favor of this type of life. The routine of the businessman's life frees him from the requirement of making unimportant, but time-consuming decisions. He does not have to decide what time to get up in the morning, what to wear, what train to take, or the like. All these decisions have been made and are part of his life. He is free then to fill his mind with more creative activities. So there can be arguments on both sides. However, if his actual occupation makes him solely a cog in a large machine so that he has no say over the functioning of that machine, then it seems fair to say that any motivation for creativity will be lost and his freed mind will be engaged in devising plans whereby he can appear to be doing a better job than the six other men in his corporation who hold similar positions. If he has grown up in middle-class America, the achievement norm has been deeply ingrained in him, and he knows that he must continue to get promotions if he is to succeed and that he must succeed if he is to be "somebody."

Without prolonging this discussion and allowing for a shortage of specific evidence on this topic, it seems quite fair to say that the bureaucratic dimension of modern society does in fact have a considerable effect on the operations of the social psychological factors discussed in this book and that social psychologists do need to give it their attention.

SUMMARY
We prefer to use the word "group" to refer to two or more people, who share common norms and whose social roles are interlocking. Although a great diversity of phenomena fit

under this heading, it does not include aggregates, in which people are together geographically but engage in little or no interaction, and it does not include those persons who share a common characteristic but do not interact. We introduced the word "category" to be used for the latter.

When analyzed in terms of the type and intensity of their internal relationships, groups can be divided into primary and secondary groups. The primary group is more intimate and lasting and involves emotional attachments, whereas the secondary group is seen mainly in terms of its practical use in helping the members move toward their individual goals.

Reference groups are those groups used by the individual as a perspective from which he looks at his perceptual world. They may or may not be groups in which he is actually a member. It is not unusual for him to use the frame or reference of the group of which he would like to be a member.

The size of the group has a considerable bearing on its functioning and its influence on the individual. When the size of a small group increases from two to three, a number of new processes come into being. When it becomes even larger, more factors must be considered. Finally, when the group gets to the size that the members cannot easily engage in face-to-face interactions with each other, we have a different type of group altogether, in which more explicit division of labor is required.

The individual's participation in a large formal bureaucracy seems to have significant consequences for the operation of social psychological factors.

SUGGESTED REFERENCES

* Caplow, Theodore: *Two against One*, Prentice-Hall, Inc., Englewood Cliffs, N.J., 1968.
Develops the idea that social interaction is always triangular because the behavior of pairs is subject to the influence of an audience.

* Cooley, Charles H.: *Social Organization* (1st ed., 1909), Schocken Books, Inc., New York, 1962.
The classic work of Cooley, in which he presents his ideas on the primary group.

* Goffman, Erving: *Encounters*, The Bobbs-Merrill Co., Inc., Indianapolis, 1961.
One of Goffman's many insightful books into the processes of interaction. (See other works cited in references section of Chapter 5.)

Hare, A. Paul: *Handbook of Small Group Research*, The Free Press, New York, 1962.
Review of most of the research material on small groups up to date of publication. Excellent reference; complete bibliography.

————, Edgar F. Borgatta, and Robert F. Bales: *Small Groups: Studies in Social Interaction*, 2d ed., Alfred A. Knopf, Inc., New York, 1965.
Excellent source for material written on small groups from an interactionist's point of view.

* Liebow, Elliot: *Tally's Corner*, Little, Brown, and Company, Boston, 1967.
An excellent ethnographic analysis of Negro street-corner men and their relationships with their children, wives, lovers, friends, and jobs.

* Olmsted, M. S.: *The Small Group*, Random House, Inc., New York, 1959.
The best short review of small-group studies available.

* Putney, Snell, and Gail J. Putney: *The Adjusted American,* Harper & Row, Publishers, New York, 1964 (Harper Torch-books).
  A clever discussion of the effect of modern society on the lives of Americans.

* Shepherd, Clovis R.: *Small Groups: Some Sociological Perspectives,* Chandler Publishing Co., San Francisco, 1964.
  A valuable review of the theory and research in the area of small groups.

Sherif, Muzafer, and Carolyn W. Sherif: *Reference Groups,* Harper & Row, Publishers, New York, 1964.
  A study of norms and behavior among a group of adolescent boys.

* Simmel, Georg: *The Sociology of Georg Simmel* (Kurt Wolff trans., ed., and intro.), The Free Press, New York, 1950.
  The pioneer work of the early sociologist who contributed much to small-group theory.

Taylor, Howard F.: *Balance in Small Groups,* Van Nostrand Reinhold Company, New York, 1970.
  A review of the contributions to balance theory and some extensions on the most valuable notions.

* Whyte, William H.: *The Organization Man,* Doubleday & Company, Inc., Garden City, N.Y., 1956.
  The now-classic work on the effects of industrial society on modern man.

* References marked with asterisk are available in paperback.

SEVEN

SIMILARITY IN GROUPS

In the last chapter, we dealt with the many and varied ways that groups might be classified. It was apparent that the different types of groups had differing effects on the members of the group. This chapter will deal with the similarities in groups—the common elements that exist in every group whether it be a street gang, a family in a preliterate society, or the board of directors of a large corporation.

STRUCTURAL DIMENSIONS OF THE GROUP

To do a social psychological analysis of a group, it is important to look at the ways that the various dimensions of the group fit today. The activity, the attitudes, and the interaction all fit together in meaningful ways. In this section, we will deal with some of the concepts needed for understanding the structure of the group.

Norms

We return now to the discussion of norms. When norms were first discussed, we defined them as those rules and standards for behavior that are shared by the members of the group or the society.

They are the expectations that members hold for each other as they interact in the group. We saw in the previous chapter that norms are a part of the definition of the group. Interaction alone does not create a group; when this interaction leads to the emergence of a set of norms, we have a group. Only then can we see the individuals as a unit, organized in some structural form. Since this concept of norms is central to the understanding of the group and its influence on the individual, a clear understanding of the concept is of the utmost importance.

We have said that group norms are the standards for behavior that the members of the group have for each other. This idea seems clear in its abstract form; but, when used in the analysis of specific instances, it is likely to become somewhat confusing. We could say that norms regulate reciprocal relations and define relevant, or appropriate, behavior. Where do the norms of the group come from? From our earlier discussion of primary groups, it should be clear that there are two sources of norms. First, the individual members of the group bring with them into the interaction setting established norms that are relevant because the group's members are also members of the society or of some larger social system. Second, some norms emerge from the interactions of the group.

An Englishman once said that if a group of Americans found themselves marooned on a desert island, the first thing they would do would be to elect a president, a vice-president, a recording secretary, a corresponding secretary, and a treasurer. What he is saying is that Americans have so internalized the cultural norms that place importance on formal structure that they may well disregard the functional effectiveness of the particular structure in fulfilling the group's goals. His story is humorous because we are aware that in the usual setting it would be expected that the needs or goals of the group would determine which norms of society are relevant and what new norms need to be established. If rational, we would not blindly follow the formal rules unless they applied to the situations or we were compelled to do so.

We might start with the principle that groups originate when a number of individuals with common goals find they cannot attain their objectives through individual efforts alone. Around these common problems, the initial interaction takes place and from them the norms emerge. Some patterns of behavior seem to work well at starting the group to move toward its goals—these are rewarded, valued, and repeated. Other acts are found to be ineffective and are discarded. From this type of exchange emerge standards for behavior. The group develops a structure and the individual members may begin to feel more comfortable as they learn what is expected of them in the group.

Roles

At the same time as some acts are seen as effective at moving the group and others are seen as ineffective, a similar process is working with regard to different individuals. As the inter-action proceeds, some participants demonstrate their resource-fulness in pursuing common goals while others show their ineptness. Those who perform well become valued members of the group and are awarded high status for their efforts. The ineffective member is likely to find himself in a low position. While this status differentiation is going on, certain members are showing proficiency in fulfilling some of the specific needs of the group, while others emerge as expert in other areas. In this way, the individuals are accorded different positions within the group, and sets of norms are established for the holders of these positions. We use the term "role" or "*role norm*" to refer to *the expectations that the group has for individuals who hold particular positions within the group.*

Position and Status

We shall distinguish between the concept of *position*, which refers to the location of an individual relative to others within a social system, and *status*, which imputes a value hierarchy in addition to location. In making this distinction, we are emphasizing two types of differentiations that occur within the group. The word "position" draws our attention to the fact that a division of labor occurs—some persons have one type of job, others have other jobs. In this concept alone, there is no connotation of value; that is, that one job is better than another. However, the word "status" does bring to bear the values that the group places on the position. The members of the group can be ranked according to their status. Our oft-used example of the family demonstrates the concept of position. When we talk about the position of the father in the family, we do not (or we need not) mean that the father is higher or lower than the wife in their relative value position (status) in the group. We use the word "father" to locate the person in the structure of the family relative to the other positions (wife and children).

Some positions, by their very nature, imply status as well. The position of leader is the prime example of this. Regarding status, it has been shown that in emerging groups the extreme status positions are allocated early, leaving the middle positions undefined or fluctuating for a prolonged period before they are finally established. In other words, that person or those persons who are most efficient and resourceful in moving the group in desired directions will soon be recognized and awarded the status of leadership. They will be looked up to; their suggestions will be honored; and they will have considerable influence in guiding the group activity. At the same time, there are likely to be those whose behavior is disruptive to the operations of the group. These persons also stand out; they too will be awarded status. But their status will be low, and they are likely to be allocated responsibilities that others do not want. Those in the middle may never be completely differentiated.

These examples imply that groups frequently emerge out of nothing. This, of course, is not true, and we must remember that every group is also a part of a larger society. If our group of Americans on the desert island consisted of twenty men and two women, who would you guess would be elected for the secretary jobs? No, they would not wait to see who could take notes or write most effectively; they would immediately elect the women. Even on the desert island, the society plays an important part in the allocation of positions within the group.

The analysis of status and position is especially clear in the study of formal organization. Consider the typical industrial organizational chart presented in Figure 5. The higher a position lies on the chart the higher the status of the incumbent of that position. At the level of the workers, there may be a number of different jobs. Some are producing the product, others assembling, others packaging, and so on. We would say that the producer, the assembly man, and the packager hold down different positions but have the same status. Note that the chart of the family structure is most valuable for depicting the location of participants relative to their interlocking roles, whereas the factory chart shows the relative status of the persons in the various positions.

This brings us to another dimension of group structure. We have already implied that there are formal and informal groups, but we have not mentioned that within the large complex organization there is always an informal organization as well as the formal structure. To use our example cited above, it well may be that among the workers other types of status differentiations exist. Formally, on the organization chart, there is no indication of difference between the assembly-line worker and the packagers; however, the workers know that the assembly operation takes considerable skill, whereas anyone can put a product in a box. Because they perceive difference in the skill required for the various tasks, they place value on these positions and thus award status to the incumbents of the various positions. In the workers' chart that they carry around in their heads, the assembly worker is placed appreciably higher than the packager.

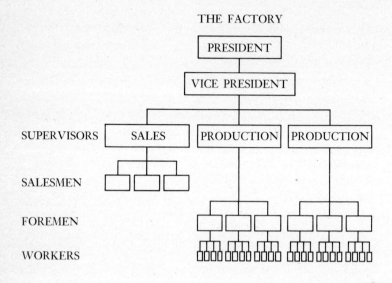

THE FACTORY

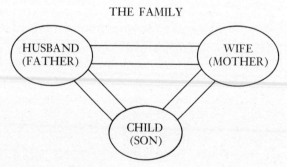

THE FAMILY

Figure 5   Two group structures.

Of course, it follows that with status come *power* and *influence*. By this we mean that the higher the person's status the more likely he is to be able to move the group activities in directions that he desires. In the small informal group, the individual who emerges as leader is also the most powerful member of the group. This relationship between power and status can be very important because it tends to stabilize the positions within the group and to make mobility (moving from one status to another) more difficult.

Remember that the individual rose to the leadership position because he was the most resourceful in helping the group to pursue its common goals. So we can say the leadership status will be awarded to persons who do what the group wants them to do—direct it toward its goal. To maintain this position of leadership, the leader must live up to the standards of behavior that the group values as well as or better than any of the other members. He is at an advantage because, in his position as leader, he has the power to maneuver the group's activities in directions that he wishes. Also he is most influential in defining the group goals. Therefore, he can lead the group in directions that permit him to demonstrate his leadership skills and away from activities in which he lacks skills. For example, a member of a street-corner gang who emerged as gang leader because his intellectual skills enabled him to out-smart or out-talk other potential leaders may take advantage of his status position to direct group activity away from athletic activities in which he might not perform well and toward activities that require more mental skill. So he persuades them to play card games that require intellectual skills rather than play baseball. This same type of dynamics may operate in large formal organizations: the newly selected president of the corporation may redirect the activity of his firm into areas in which he has special expertise, thereby making his skills necessary for the continued operation of the company.

STRUCTURAL NETWORKS

The one important characteristic of a group that differentiates it from a simple collection of people is that the group is *organized*. There is a pattern to the behavior of the indi-

viduals; they do not simply act at random or in accordance
with their individual needs or feelings. They act in regard to
each other according to established and organized standards.
To put it another way, the group has *structure*. When the
social psychologist talks about *group structure,* he is referring
to *shared norms and the distinguishable parts or positions, and
their arrangement with respect to each other, that identify the
group as an independent entity.* A group is highly structured
when there is complete or nearly complete consensus on the
norms, roles, and values of the group that clearly define the
arrangement of relationships. On the other hand, an unstructured group would be demonstrated by the situation in which
there is little agreement as to what is expected of the group
members (the norms and roles). Of course, a completely
unstructured group is an impossibility, since it could not fit
the minimum criteria for our definition of the group.

Note that when we use the concept structure we are talking
about something quite different from formality. Structure
refers to the degree of consensus on the norms and roles,
whereas formality refers to the implicit or explicit formulation
of these norms and roles. Although formal groups or organizations tend to be more highly structured, some informal
groups are also highly structured. A street-corner gang that
has existed over a period of years may have very rigid standards and practices that all the members agree must be lived up
to, even though they are seldom mentioned and no one would
consider writing them down.

Social Control

What makes persons conform to the norms of the group or
the society? Of course, they do not always conform, but for
the most part they do. To answer this question, we must deal
with *social control,* that is, *the mechanisms that operate within
the group to insure conformity on the part of the members.*
First of all, we can see that a reasonably high degree of con-

formity is necessary in order for the group or the society to function. We do not usually think of language as a set of norms; but, as we learned under that heading, language can be seen as shared agreements to use words in a particular way. This means that language is part of the normative structure of the group. What if the participants refused to use the language? Well, of course there would be no communication and, in a short time, no group. So we can say that people conform to norms in order to maintain the existence of the group. However, some participants may violate some of the norms, at least some of the time, without destroying or even seriously impairing the operation of the group. So the group or society develops methods to encourage members to conform and to discourage nonconformity.

In the primary group, when a person does not conform to the norms, the other members have considerable influence over him because of his emotional commitment to the group. The threat of a breakdown in his relationship with the group may be enough in itself to keep him in conformity. Then, too, he is not likely to voluntarily violate a norm of the primary group, because he feels that he is a member of the group and conforming to the group norms is part of being a member. In the secondary group, in which concern is not so much with the relationship with the other members as it is with the practical matter of what the group has set out to accomplish, the individual is motivated to conform by his concern for accomplishing the end that he joined the group for. One of the norms of the secondary group in the barber shop, for example, is that the customer will sit in the barber chair without getting up and walking around until his haircut has been completed. He conforms to this norm because he knows that he will not get what he came in for—a haircut—if he does not.

Remember that most people adhere to the norms of their groups because they want to, because they feel that conformity is the proper way of getting along with those about them

and accomplishing their ends. Not all persons conform. Sometimes persons learn the norms of the group only by experienc-
ing the reactions directed at them when their behavior is not in
conformity with the norms. *Those reactions that the group
directs toward the individual member to encourage him to
conform to the group are called sanctions.*

A sanction may take the form of a reward for conforming
behavior or a punishment for nonconformity. When a new
member comes into the group he is likely to be consciously
asking himself, "How am I expected to behave?" He will
observe the behavior of others, but most importantly he will
observe the way others are responding to each other. That is,
he will be looking to see which actions are rewarded and
which actions require punishment. By observing how the
sanctions are administered, he will acquire a picture of what
the group norms are and thus what will be expected of him.

On the level of society, we sometimes divide up norms in
terms of the severity of the sanctions that would be directed at
the nonconformist. *Folkways* are those regulatory norms, such
as etiquette, that are not important to the survival of the group
or society and are likely to be met with casual sanctions such
as a frown directed at a person who eats with the wrong
utensil. On the other hand, *mores* are those more important
norms that reflect the values of the society or group and that
demand a more severe response to violation. In our society, the
commission of a crime such as robbery would be a clear
example of the violation of its mores. Our society highly
values personal property and places great importance on non-
violence. When a member of our society steals property from
the person of another with the threat of doing bodily harm
(that is, when a robbery takes place), the robber is violating
several valued norms of the society. The law sets the sanction.
A person convicted of first-degree robbery in California shall
be imprisoned in the state penitentiary for from five years to
life.

When the mores of a group are violated, the punishment is likely to take the form of ostracism from the group. If a group of scientists working together on a project find that one of their members is making up his results rather than performing experiments (intellectual honesty is highly valued among scientists), he is likely to be dropped from their team. The reader has probably noted, from our two examples of sanctions applied to mores, that the action taken against the violating individual is not always directed at getting *him* back into the lines of conformity within the specific group or society. A man who has to spend ten years in prison will not have much chance to show that he has learned his lesson, and the banned scientist is not in a position to do his experiments the way he should have in the first place. These sanctions operate more as examples to others in defining for them what is expected of the group and demonstrating the importance that the group places on conformity to these mores.

The division of norms into folkways and mores is potentially misleading if it is taken to suggest that there are two qualitatively different types of norms. Norms and their corresponding sanctions vary in terms of the value placed on conformity and the severity of the sanctions. Note also that the types of sanction that are available to the group vary considerably from one group to another. The refusal of a group of students to let one of their members remain in their group because he uses language they find offensive may be of little consequence to either the group, which has plenty of members, or to the individual, who can find another group to have coffee with. But a family decision to drop one of their children because he continually misbehaves would be a different matter. The operations of norm and sanction in a group like the family take on quite a different flavor from those of the casual informal group of students.

Why do we conform? Why would we expect to find similar behavior, attitudes, and opinions among members of a group?

We can suggest three plausible explanations: (1) Membership in the group determines for an individual many of the things he learns and therefore only a limited range of alternatives is open to him (this is particularly true of the child in the family). (2) The group member may identify with the group, be glad to be a member, and conform to the norms because he wants to or because he sees the group, and conformity to its expectations, as a way to get to his personal goals. (3) A person may behave in conformity with the norms of his group because he is afraid of the punishment, ridicule, or rejection that the group members may impose upon him if he fails to conform.

To assure that an individual will conform to a particular norm, sometimes the situation is such that the group can teach the individual only one way of behaving and thus not let him know it is possible to deviate. If this procedure is not workable (and it usually is not), the group must decide between the other two—getting the individual to identify with the group so that he wants to conform to the norms or threatening him with punishment if he deviates. Available evidence seems to suggest that, when plausible, the first of these two measures is more effective. For example, at a large university the fraternities tried various ways to get their pledges to conform to the norms that their fraternities set forth for them. During a period of harassment (hell week), when the pledges were kept awake most of the night, they were still expected to stay awake during their classes and study hours. The various fraternities used different measures to assure conformity to the nonsleeping norm. One group used the identification method, by telling their members that they were now becoming members of the honored fraternity of Alpha Alpha and that as good members they would be expected to live up to the high expectations of this body. They would be expected to make every effort to keep themselves awake. The other group of fraternities took the punishment approach. They told their pledges that they would be watched in their classes and study hours and that, if they were caught sleeping, they would be punished for their violations. An observer who was studying these practices interviewed the pledges afterwards. Those who were left on their honor claimed that they made every effort to keep awake, including taking pep pills. The other men who were threatened by punishment felt that, as long as they were assured of not getting caught, it was all right to sleep and reported that they made efforts to elude the eyes of the active fraternity members and sneak off and sleep. The first method proved far more effective.

Child psychologists tell us approximately the same thing in suggesting that positive reinforcement (rewarding desired behavior) is far more effective than negative sanctions (punishing undesirable behavior). However, it is not always possible to wait for the desirable behavior, and every group at one time or another uses both types of responses to encourage its members to conform to the group norms.

A word should be said about the practice of conformity. It has become fashionable in some segments of our society to hold the conformist in disdain and to hold the nonconformist in high regard. Nonconformity becomes a norm. The nonconformist becomes a conformist, which appears to be a contradiction. This situation can be untangled by two observations. First, those who support the norm of nonconformity will expect their norm to apply only in certain areas of life. Usually, theirs is a position more against the strict and stifling conformity of a bureaucratic society where creativity is lost because of extreme demands of uniformity, than one that encourages complete uniqueness of behavior.

A second factor that must be considered is that very possibly what is conformity to one group is nonconformity to another. Behavior that the larger society may deem nonconformity and in violation of its norms may be conformity to the norms of the individual's group. In Chapter 10, this and other forms of deviancy will be dealt with in detail.

Conflicting Norms and Roles

This brings us to another topic of interest to the social psychologist. Up to the last paragraph, the discussion of norms and social control might be interpreted as implying that groups never cross and that group norms were always a reflection of the norms of society. Of course, we know better. The boy who is a member of a delinquent gang may learn early in his life that stealing is an expected way of life on the street. Evidence indicates that stealing among lower-class gang members is not simply a matter of the child's desire to acquire material objects that are not accessible to him because of his deprived position in society. This form of behavior seems rather to be a deliberate attempt to show his defiance of the larger society's (middle-class) values, which place importance on material goods.

This is not the only type of role-conflict that we are likely to run into. Remember that the term "role" has been used to refer to the expectations that are directed at a person by the members of his group or society because of a position he holds or a characteristic he possesses. Because we all have a number of characteristics and positions, it is not unusual that a person is called upon to enact more than one role at a time—a student, a girl, a chairman of a committee are positions that one person might be required to hold at the same time. Usually this multiplicity of roles creates no particular problem. We are used to multiple-role situations. However, on occasion, the role-expectation for one position conflicts with the requirements for another. Consider the student who is asked by the instructor to proctor an examination in which some of his friends are students. What does he do when he observes one of his friends cheating on the exam? In the position as proctor his role is

clear. He must report the cheating. In his position as friend
the norm is closer to "You don't squeal on your friends." So he
is in a dilemma and must choose which role he prefers to adhere to. This is the type of role-conflict in which the individual finds himself the member of two groups at the same
time and finds in a particular situation that those two groups
have opposing expectations for him.

There are some positions in our society that almost always
have conflicting aspects to them. This is usually due to the fact
that the group itself does not agree upon the expectation for
the particular position. The foreman in industry is a classic
example. He is almost always selected from among the
workers, so he may have a primary relationship with them. But
he is selected by the management to be their representative to
the workers. He is called upon to distribute the work and see
to it that the task at hand is completed according to management's specifications. The tasks are not equally desirable, and
he is in a position to do favors for his friends. If he does, he
will be violating the expectations of the management; if he
does not, his friends will dislike him. It is not at all unusual for
a workman to refuse a promotion to foreman because he is
aware of the conflicts that are inherent in the position.

Still another type of conflict is brought about by society's
lack of consensus about the role for a particular position or
characteristic. This is most true during a period of rapid social
change. An excellent example of this is the position of the
woman in our society. The topic has received a great deal of
attention in recent years and will continue to in the foreseeable
future. In some ways, girls are treated as intellectual equals
with boys throughout their academic careers (with the exception of vocational training, such as business and medicine). As
a matter of fact, in high school and to some degree in college,
they are expected to do better than men in some subjects
(English, social studies, but not math). High school grades are
consistently higher for girls than for boys, and the academic

success of women in college even through graduate school is likely to equal or surpass that of the men. When women leave the educational institution and go out to find employment, they find that it is a man's world. They were at one time taught that they were the equal of men, but they find that another segment of society considers them quite inferior. It now becomes apparent to the young lady why she was advised to "act dumb" on her dates. If the girl who completed her Ph.D. at a given university came seeking a faculty position, she would find that the same professors who taught her that she was equal to the male students feel quite different toward her as a potential colleague. It is not uncommon for a department of a college to have more than half its graduate student women and yet not have one woman on its faculty.

Thus we can see that there are a number of different ways we may get caught in role conflicts. However, when one considers the complexity of society, it seems remarkable that we are able to avoid conflicts as much as we do.

Cohesiveness

We turn now to a concept that refers to a property or characteristic of the group; that is, it cannot be seen in terms of the individuals making up the group, but only as descriptive of the group as a whole. The term *cohesiveness* will be used to refer to *the forces that operate on the members of the group to make them stick together and remain members of the group.* This is a perplexing concept, since it has many dimensions and has been approached from a number of directions by social psychologists. If the student can remember that the literal meaning of the word "cohesive" is "sticking together," he will have a pretty good idea of what we are talking about. When we ask how cohesive a group is, we are asking to what degree do the members stick together.

A number of other words in common usage refer approximately to the same notion. "Morale," "esprit de corps," "we-feeling" all have similar meanings but have additional connotations that may be misleading. One study observed the number of times the word "we" was used versus "I" as individuals described their activities in the group. It does seem to make sense that in a highly cohesive group the members are more likely to see themselves as part of the group as a whole and to make reference to "we" rather than "they" or "I."

Other dimensions of cohesiveness might be considered. A group would be said to be cohesive if the members all worked together for a common goal or, similarly, if each was ready and willing to take responsibility for group tasks. On another dimension, we could say that a group is cohesive if the group members are willing to endure pain or frustration for the group and its members. A reflection of the cohesiveness of the group might be seen in the members' willingness to defend their group against external criticism or attack.

Groups, like individuals, have characteristics that differentiate them one from the other. Not all groups are equally cohesive. Some have a large turnover in membership and last only a short duration. Others seem to go on and on, with all members striving to maintain their membership. How do some groups come to have high cohesiveness and some low? Perhaps this can be answered by considering the reasons why groups are formed in the first place, since it follows logically that some degree of cohesiveness must be present for the group to come into being and maintain its existence over any period of time. Cartwright and Zander[1] suggest that an individual is attracted to a group for two sets of reasons: "(a) Such properties of the group as its goals, programs, size, type of organization, and position in the community; and (b) the needs of the person for affiliation, recognition, security, and other things which can be mediated by groups." So we see that both the nature of

[1] Dorwin Cartwright and Alvin Zander (eds.), *Group Dynamics*, Harper & Row, Publishers, New York, 1952, p. 76.

the group and the motivation of the individual go into determining how the individual sees the group. The better the group can provide for the individual's needs, the more attractive it will be for him. Thus cohesiveness cannot be seen solely in terms of what the group has to offer to the individual members but must be seen as an interaction of what the group offers and what the members need. A group becomes highly cohesive only when the right combination of members come together with the right combination of group features. This does not mean that the group must provide the same need fulfillment for each of the members. One member may need information that can be provided only by the group, while another may need the satisfaction that he has something worthwhile to give to others. A discussion group brings these two together so that the one can get the information he needs, while the other receives praise from the group for the information he contributes. This oversimplified example demonstrates that individual needs (information and reassurance) are fulfilled by the particular feature of the group (its discussion format), and therefore we would expect a cohesive group.

We would expect the members of a cohesive group to have a high level of motivation directed at responsible and enthusiastic participation in group activity. The members would exhibit a high attraction to the group, which would help in coordinating the efforts of the members. So we could summarize this discussion by saying that the consequence of cohesiveness is a happy, active, and efficient group, in which the members operate as a unit. This is the ideal. All groups fall short to greater or lesser degrees.

INTERGROUP RELATIONS

We have been talking about the characteristics within the group that hold it together. We turn now to the relationships that exist between groups. First, we must say a word about the term "intergroup relations." Unfortunately, this term has been used in a limited fashion and with connotations that may be misleading to our discussion. Frequently, when we hear the term "intergroup relations," we think of race relations and, perhaps just as often, it brings to mind racial conflict. This is unfortunate, because there is a great deal more that should be covered under this heading, a great deal that has nothing to do with either race or conflict. For our purpose, let us use the concept to refer to *the relations that exist between two or more groups and their respective members*. The technical definition of group excludes most racial factors, since in most contexts race is dealt with as a category or classification of an individual characteristic, not of a group. However, this is reconciled somewhat by the fact that many of the generalizations that can be made about intergroup relations are also appropriate for intercategory understandings.

When two groups confront each other, one of the major factors that must be considered is the perceptions that the group members have of each other. One central generalization goes a long way toward explaining intergroup relations: *When an outsider perceives the members of a particular group, he is likely to see them as relatively undifferentiated in terms of their attitudes, opinions, characteristics, behavior, and positions within the group.* If we can use the term "in-group" to refer to the group under analysis and "out-group" to refer to those looking on, we would say that the in-group perceives its membership as being differentiated on opinions and attitudes, as well as characteristics and behavior, and divides its members into positions and statuses and thus ascribes differential expectations for the membership. When viewing the in-group, the out-group is likely to perceive a homogeneous membership, all with similar characteristics. Members of the out-group recognize the leader of the in-group and perhaps a few of the high-status members. In addition, they may recognize that a particular member holds a low-status position within the group, but the members in the middle remain undifferentiated for the outsider looking in. The group is likely to become identified by the out-group with its leader, and the individual members of the group are likely to be seen as holding attitudes and values similar to those ascribed to the leader. The group is responded to without the refined differentiation that exists within the group. So when an adolescent gang feels that it would like to get together with another gang to play a game of baseball, they will communicate with the leader and make negotiations through him for the encounter. There will be little contact with other members of the group.

This perception that one group has of the other also applies to an individual outsider's perception of a group. It certainly is true, as we have seen, that group membership affects perception by causing members to be sensitive to the same cues and thus have similar perception. However, when the individual is confronted with a group that he is observing from the outside, his limited information and insights are likely to lead him to making generalizations about all the members of the group based on his perception of only a few.

What this means for the individual group member is that he is likely to be responded to by nonmembers in terms of his group identification rather than on the basis of his individual behavior, attitude, or feeling. Of course, there are some grounds for this way of responding to group members because we know that they are likely to share characteristics with the other group members. However, this can be most misleading if the out-group misperceives the in-group to begin with.

At this point, we can see the similarity between intergroup relationships and intercategory understanding. The outsider sees a person as a member of a category in much the same way that he sees him as a member of a group. That is, if he sees him as a member of the Forty-fifth Street gang, he will respond to him as if he had the characteristics that he perceives as typical of that group. In similar fashion, if he sees an individual as a member of the black race, he will respond to him as if he has the characteristics that he feels are descriptive of the black race. It is worthwhile to consider this factor in terms of the difference between groups and categories. Remember that the group is defined in terms of the interaction of the members with each other. In addition, it is usually true that group membership has more of a voluntary dimension than does membership in a category. In other words, the individual chooses to become a member of the group but has no choice as to what his race is. For this reason, groups do tend to be more homogeneous. The individual chooses the group because he sees its members as having attitudes, values, and the like, similar to his own—he sees the other members as sharing some of his feelings. Once he is in the group, the interaction among members tends to bring them together even more. On the other hand, the person who falls into the category of being black (or female or old or whatever) does not join this category because he shares views with others who have the same characteristics. He has no choice. As a possesser of that characteristic, he will not necessarily interact with others who share with him in this regard. The one thing that could move the holders of these specific characteristics together is the fact that they share a common response from outsiders. All women share the role-conflicts (to a greater or lesser degree) that we discussed in an earlier section and therefore are likely to share a number of similar feelings and attitudes, but this remains only superficial unless their common plight leads them to join in prolonged group membership.

We might conclude from this that the practice of perceiving the members of the group as holding similar values, attitudes, and opinions is probably a realistic way of responding to the situation in which individual characteristics are not available. When you confront an individual and all you know about him is that he is a member of a particular group, it is fair to assume that he holds the values and attitudes of that group (assuming that you have an accurate perception of the group's values). Does the same thing hold for categories? Probably not. It would be much more precarious to assume that all members of a particular race held the same values, and to respond to an individual solely on the basis of his race could prove unfortunate.

Turning our attention now to intergroup relations between two or more small groups, it is possible to use the above discussion of perception in understanding the relationship that we would expect to develop. First, we must note that the two groups are always part of a larger social context, which cannot be ignored in our analysis. If we are considering two delinquent gangs, we should not overlook the common relationships the groups have with the police in the area or the school authorities, or the like. If we are studying the relationships between work groups in a factory, we must see them as part of a larger structure that imposes regulations on them and limits their range of response. Considering these factors brings to light the fact that most often when groups interact they are very similar in character. That is, we are not likely to have the delinquent gang interacting with the work group; we are more likely to find it interacting with another gang. For this reason, the groups are likely to be fulfilling similar needs for their members and, in some instances, to be competing for the same potential members. Over a period of time, the two groups are likely to develop rather clear pictures of each other. One group will come to think of the other in certain prescribed ways that reflect the joint evaluations of the group members. In other words, the attitudes that one group holds toward the other will become an integral part of the group's norms.

In such a setting, it is not unusual for a group with a negative evaluation of an out-group to perceive threats, unjust treatment, or invasion of their rights by this rival out-group. This tends to crystallize opinions and to cause the in-group to develop measures for defending itself against the out-group. It is a well-established fact that, *when a group is attacked from the outside, the cohesiveness within the group increases.* Hostility toward an out-group resulting from competition and rivalry is very likely to lead to cooperation and solidarity *within* the in-group. Petty intragroup differences are forgotten, and the members work together against their common enemy.

The social psychologist Muzafer Sherif,[2] in his famous study of intergroup relations, went a step further. He asked, "How can two groups in conflict be brought into harmony?" After experimenting on a number of factors with boys at a series of summer camps set up for research purposes, he concluded that "the possibilities for achieving harmony are greatly enhanced when groups are brought together to work toward common ends." Hostility gives way when groups pull together to achieve overriding goals that are real and compelling to all concerned. In Sherif's experiments, the groups were provided with situations in which group goals were established that could not be obtained without the cooperation of the rival group. Then each group took a new look at the other, changed their group norms to see the other group in a more favorable light, and reduced the hostility that had existed between them and the other group.

By combining the points made in the last two paragraphs, it is possible to make one more point about intergroup relations. When two groups are jointly attacked by a third outside force, they react in a fashion similar to the dynamic described by Sherif. That is, the attack provides motivation for the groups to work together, to see each other in a new light, and to reduce hostility between them. When the street gangs are attacked by the police, they may join forces and reduce intergroup tension. If the work groups in the factory feel that they

---

[2] Muzafer Sherif and Carolyn W. Sherif, *Groups in Harmony and Tension,* Harper & Row, Publishers, New York, 1953.

are being unjustly treated by management, they may stop competing with each other and cooperate in a common effort to settle their conflict with management.

SUMMARY

In this chapter we have focused on the structure and properties of groups. We have discussed the importance of understanding the norms, roles, positions, and status differentiations that exist in every group. We considered the means used by a group to make certain that its members conform to the norms that the group has established. This led to a discussion of cohesiveness, or the factors that attract individuals to the group and hold it together once it is formed. In the final section, we discussed the question of intergroup relations. Note that the general principles set forth in this chapter, with some few exceptions, would pertain to a greater or lesser degree to every group. No group is without norms, roles, positions, sanctions, cohesiveness, and the like. These factors make all groups similar.

SUGGESTED REFERENCES

Berg, I. A., and B. M. Bass (eds.): *Conformity and Deviation*, Harper & Row, Publishers, New York, 1961.
A series of papers on various aspects of norms, authority, and conformity-deviation.

Cartwright, Dorwin, and Alvin Zander (eds.): *Group Dynamics*, 3d ed., Harper & Row, Publishers, New York, 1968.
Collection of readings in group research, generally from the field theory orientation. The editors' introductions to each section are excellent statements of the various aspects of group dynamics.

* Cooley, Charles H.: *Social Organization* (1st ed., 1909), Schocken Books, Inc., New York, 1962.
Cooley expands his theories of social psychology.

Dewey, John: *Human Nature and Conduct*, Holt, Rinehart & Winston, Inc., New York, 1922.
Dewey's classic treatise on the place of reflective thought in the organization of human behavior.

Gross, Neal, Ward S. Mason, and Alexander McEachern: *Explorations in Role Analysis*, John Wiley & Sons, Inc., New York, 1958.
Excellent conceptual development of the notions of role and positions applied to an empirical study.

Hollander, E. P. (ed.): *Leaders, Groups and Influence*, Oxford University Press, New York, 1964.
Studies of leadership, interaction, and motivation, including sociometric approaches.

Homans, George: *The Human Group*, Harcourt Brace Jovanovich, Inc., New York, 1950.
Excellent synthesis of studies on the human group.

————: *Social Behavior: Its Elementary Forms*, Harcourt Brace Jovanovich, Inc., New York, 1961.

A detailed description of many of the forms of social behavior considered in this chapter.

Petrullo, L., and B. M. Bass (eds.): *Leadership and Interpersonal Behavior*, Holt, Rinehart & Winston, Inc., New York, 1961. Collection of papers on leadership, with emphasis on diverse theoretical formulations.

* Presthus, Robert: *Men at the Top*, Oxford University Press, New York, 1964.
Analysis of power and influence in the community setting.

* Sherif, Muzafer: *The Psychology of Social Norms*, Harper & Row, Publishers, 1966 (Harper Torchbooks).
An unusually suggestive study in which the principles of normative behavior are shown to be most valuable in accounting for man's behavior.

————— (ed.): *Intergroup Relations and Leadership*, John Wiley & Sons, Inc., 1962.
Studies of leadership in industrial, ethnic, and political segments of contemporary society.

Shibutani, Tamotsu: *Society and Personality*, Prentice-Hall, Inc., Englewood Cliffs, N.J., 1961.
An interactionist approach to social psychology. One of the best treatments of the group from this point of view.

Short, James F., and Fred L. Strodtbeck: *Group Process and Gang Delinquency*, The University of Chicago Press, Chicago, 1965.
Application by sociologists of some concepts of group process to the study of delinquent gangs.

* References marked with asterisk are available in paperback.

EIGHT

SOCIALIZATION

We have emphasized throughout this book the importance of recognizing the social nature of man. Nowhere is this more apparent than in the study of socialization. *Socialization* refers to *the process whereby the individual learns the habits, beliefs, and standards for behavior and judgment that make him identifiable as a member of the group or society.* Most discussions of socialization concern themselves almost exclusively with childhood socialization. We shall go extensively into this topic in the first part of this chapter but shall also discuss socialization after childhood, thus recognizing the fact that any transition into any new group requires a period of socialization wherein the new member learns those things expected of him as a member of that particular group.

CHILDHOOD SOCIALIZATION

In order to learn the habits, beliefs, and standards for behavior, the child must have certain equipment—both social and biological—that are prerequisites for that level of learning. Social skills like role-taking and linguistic skills are necessary for complete socialization. Yet they are so much a part of childhood socialization itself that we do not always distinguish between the acquisition of these skills and the learning of the culture, that is, socialization. This is understandable, since once we know how the child acquires language and role-taking ability, there is little to add in order to understand how he acquires the norms, values, and attitudes that make up the content of socialization. Therefore, a good portion of what follows might in the strict sense be called the preparation for socialization.

Biological Influences

In the simplest of terms, we are asking the question: How does a newborn child become an adult member of society? We reject the notion that he just grows up. The complex forms of social behavior in which he engages as an adult cannot be accounted for in terms of physical and biological maturation. The very definition that we have stated above suggests that the habits, beliefs, and standards that make an individual identifiable as a member of society come about through some type of *learning* process. If it is agreed that learning refers to those relatively permanent changes in the organism's behavior or response tendencies that result from *experience*, then we can see that socialization accounts for all the individual's behavior that is not a direct biological response of the organism to organic demands.

Is it relevant to ask the old questions of heredity versus environment? We know from the studies of lower animals that tremendously complex forms of behavior can be explained only in terms of unlearned, inborn instincts. For example, when a female rat becomes pregnant she instinctively constructs a nest for her expected offspring. Even though she has never seen this done by other rats or done it herself, she sets to work putting sticks and twigs together to form the nest. Experimental psychologists describe the pregnant rat in a cage where no nest-building materials are available: she picks up her tail, carries it across the cage, and lays it in place to start a nest. Instinct is clearly a strong factor in motivating the behavior of lower animals. Does it follow that humans must therefore have instincts? Not necessarily.

First, the identification of instincts in humans, if they did exist, would be much more difficult than is the case with lower animals. Humans do not exhibit any gross forms of behavior that clearly cannot be attributed to learning, such as in the case of the migration of birds. The human being is a social animal. He spends so much of his first years of life in a state of dependency on other humans that no behavior pattern can be assumed to be instinctive. It is possible to take a newborn rat and place it in an isolated cage where it has no contact with other rats, except for a very short interval when it becomes pregnant, and observe its nest-building behavior with complete assurance that the behavior under observation was completely unlearned. But can we do this with humans? Of course not. Ethical considerations within our society forbid the social psychologist from experimenting on humans in this fashion no matter how important some may feel it is to know the conse- quences of the relative importances of heredity versus en- vironment.

However, this does not mean that we are completely with- out any evidence whatsoever. The evidence is admittedly poor, but there are a few studies of children who have been found after they have been brought up for a period of time in conditions of isolation. Kingsley Davis[1] reports a significant case of this type. A girl by the name of Isabelle, an illegitimate child, was discovered at the age of six and a half after a life of virtual isolation in a single room with her deaf-mute mother. When first observed, her behavior was described as similar to that of a wild animal, filled with fear and hostility. She did not

[1] Kingsley Davis, "Final Note on a Case of Extreme Isolation," *American Journal of Sociology*, vol. 52, no. 5, pp. 432–437, 1947.

speak but made strange croaking sounds. In many ways, she acted like an infant. What is more significant is the report of the psychologist who examined her, which suggests that she was apparently unaware of relationships of any kind. It was some time before it was possible to determine whether she could hear, for she was unresponsive to sounds. When she was first tested, it was thought that Isabelle was probably feeble-minded and uneducable; however, when subjected to systematic training, she made considerable progress. It took a week before she made her first attempt at vocalization, but within two months she was putting sentences together and in nine months she could write reasonably well. At fourteen years of age, she was almost on a par with her age-mates, having passed the sixth grade in a public school; and she was acting like a normal child.

Unfortunately, the stories of Isabelle and others like her do not tell us much about the role of instincts in accounting for human behavior. What they do suggest is that the lack of social relations and particularly the lack of opportunity to learn language behavior create serious impairments in mental functioning.

From this we are led away from the questions of heredity and environment to a more meaningful question: Given certain biological potentials, how do the experiences of the individual and his social interaction mold him into a human adult? Apparently, there are three elements of growth needed for the development of a healthy and normal adult personality: (1) a physiological mechanism of great complexity and without serious neurological or glandular defects, (2) membership in a coherent and functioning society, and (3) a long history of apprenticeship in primary groups exerting some degree of harmonious and consistent influences of informal social control.

Perhaps the role of biological factors can be more clearly understood by considering some of the needs of the individual that appear to be obviously biological in origin. There is no argument that the individual needs food, water, and air; he needs to sleep; and, although some might care to debate the question, he probably needs some kind of sexual outlet. These are clearly universal factors, existing in every society. They appear to be unlearned, innate responses to physiological demands. Take a careful look at them. How much of your behavior can be accounted for by a recognition of these needs? Does your need for food help to explain why you buy a hamburger when you are hungry, rather than attack your fellow student to get his lunch? What we are suggesting here is that these basic biological needs function to put the organism into a state of general tension, but it is only through his social experiences that the individual learns to direct his behavior toward a satisfactory resolution to the problem, or reduction of the need. Furthermore, the amount of one's behavior that has its origin in the tensions aroused by these basic biological needs is only a small proportion of all of the activity that an individual engages in during the course of an average day. Most of his behavior cannot be attributed to biological factors.

At birth, the child is equipped with a variety of what we might call reflexes, which enable him to maintain life. He can breathe, suck, digest his food, and so on. His motor activity and his crying seem to be quite random and unpatterned at first. It is not possible to determine if his cry is in response to pain, hunger, or general discomfort. The clear tendency to be active started before his birth and continues in a relatively undifferentiated fashion for some time after he is born. With this as the starting point, we must now look at the environmental factors and particularly at the social factors that mold him into a human adult.

Preparation for Language

If we take the child born into the world with a physiological mechanism functioning properly, what accounts for his developing the way he does? First, remember that he is born with a general tendency to be active. As any mother knows, his movements start long before birth, and his vocal apparatus, which is operative at birth, is active for long periods of times during the first days of the child's life. These first movements and sounds seem to be more random than patterned. Our first question is: How do these random movements become directed into patterned behavior forms? The answer to this question calls upon the classic learning theory developed by the behaviorists in psychology. The behaviorists argue that learning takes place when a response to a drive stimulus is reinforced by the reduction of the drive. In the simplest terms, when a person is hungry (drive stimulus) and he eats dinner, his hunger will be reduced (reinforcement). By connecting the drive (hunger) with the response (eating), he has learned to reduce the drive.

Applying this principle to our newborn child, we have a beginning for an explanation for early learning. Let us say that a diaper pin is pricking the baby. According to our earlier observation this stimulus can lead only to a random response. It puts the organism in a state of tension. The child cries and wildly moves his arms and legs. During this series of random movements, he may well move to a position in which the pin is no longer hurting him. The stimulus drive is reduced, and that particular response is rewarded. The child may not learn the first time, but eventually he may make the connection between the response and the reduction of the need and we can say that elementary learning is taking place. This very simplified example should not lead the student to feel that this process is straightforward and completely understood by social psychologists. In a more complex situation, there may be a number of satisfactory solutions, and the behavior patterns that develop within the child become some type of preferential selection. One of the solutions is chosen, repeated, and eventually becomes incorporated as habitual behavior for the child. From what can be observed, the selection takes place on the basis of expediency. The child does the things that are gratifying to him and rejects those that result in pain. This hedonistic pain-and-pleasure explanation appears to give us the best explanation for this earlier behavior on the part of the child, even though there are many situations in which we cannot explain why some things seem to be pleasant for the child and other things appear to be painful. The behaviorists' explanation is that the one response is drive reducing and the other is either neutral or tension creating. Of course, in examples like the child being fed, it is easy to argue that the intake of food is tension reducing and therefore gratifying for the child. This brings up another important principle that we must borrow from the behaviorists. The newborn child gives certain reflexive responses to stimuli that come in or near his mouth. He will suck on his hand, his mother's breast, a play toy, or a bottle. But only certain ones of these objects lead to gratification of his need for food and he soon learns to distinguish between those that do and those that do not, so that later the sight of the bottle or the mother will bring forth in the child the same response as was derived from drinking milk. If each time the child sees a bottle he gets fed, the relationship between the bottle and the pleasure will be reinforced. In the same way, the mother becomes a source of pleasure for him because she is identified with the original tension reduction. The process whereby new stimuli are attached to old responses is called conditioning. The intake of food was an unconditioned stimulus that caused the child to respond (feel pleasure), but since the mother and the bottle were present whenever the food intake occurred the child learned to relate them (the conditioned stimuli) with the response. Later, when one of the conditioned stimuli was present (the mother) without the unconditioned stimulus (milk), the baby still responded by feeling pleasure. This response is now referred to as the conditioned response, since it is elicited by a new stimulus.

We are not attempting to explain all human behavior through a theory of stimulus-response conditioning. We are saying that some of the initial behavioral patterns that develop in the child can best be explained by this formulation. It is particularly useful in accounting for the acquisition of language, which is central to our understanding of the process of socialization.

Acquisition of Language

The first vocalization of the child comes almost immediately after birth. The birth-cry indicates to the mother that the child is alive and breathing. However, like the early motor responses, these early cries are reflexes, completely physiological responses to tension states of the body. It is not unusual for laymen and particularly parents to interpret these cries as expressions of emotions or of responses to particular stimuli; however, there is nothing specific about them. In one study in which movies of one-month-old babies crying were shown to parents, it was impossible for the parents to determine if the cries were a response to hunger, pain, or cold. The cries varied in intensity, but in no other way.

This state does not last long. By the time the child is about three months of age he is likely to be making all sorts of sounds. The child psychologists tell us that the range of vocalizations for children at this age, regardless of their race or nationality, is wider than it will be later in adult life—we customarily utilize only a restricted segment of the possible variations in sounds. This period is sometimes referred to as the babbling and cooing stage, since the child seems to enjoy hearing himself and is likely to spend long playful periods in which he learns to repeat the same sounds over and over again.

This babbling is of key importance because the child is learning self-imitation, which will provide the basis for later imitation of the speech of older persons around him. It seems reasonable to explain self-imitation in much the same way as we explained other types of learning. The child makes these various and somewhat random sounds, but some sounds seem more pleasurable to him than others. Some are unpleasant. Through the stimulus-response connections he learns to repeat some sounds and to ignore or extinguish others. He has learned to imitate himself.

But this is a long way from using language in a meaningful way. He next must learn to imitate the sounds of his associates. This usually begins at about nine months of age. (The ages at which children reach these various stages vary considerably among perfectly normal children. Here we present nine months as the average age at which imitating of adults begins; however, it is not unusual for one child to show the first signs of imitation at six months, while another will not appear to be imitating until he is more than a year old. Neither is exceptional.) Remember that at this new stage of development, most children have been making a wide assortment of sounds for some time. The parents or other adults attending to the child during this period frequently hear noises that they identify as being close to words. "Mama," "Dada," and "bebe" are frequently picked out by the child's elders and repeated back to him over and over again. Sometimes the sounds are repeated back and forth if the child has said the word just as the adult says it. More often there is some discrepancy. The child cannot at this stage immediately imitate his adult companion, but he has had plenty of experience making sounds and so he starts off making all sorts of sounds resembling those he has heard from the adult. Then by chance he comes upon a sound that to him is very similar to the sound he has heard from the adult. From the skills he has learned in self-imitation, he can now repeat this new sound and make it part of his repertoire. In this way he begins to imitate the simple sounds made by adults. His actions are rewarded and reinforced when the delighted adults respond favorably to his "first words" by giving him attention, picking him up, and so on.

But making sounds is not speech. Next the child must make the momentous discovery that things have names. But, curiously enough, just as important in this significant step toward conventional adult speech is the discovery that *names* have *things*. At the same time that he is learning that a particular round object is named a ball, he is learning that the word that he has been repeating for some time now—"mama"—refers to the object or person who has been taking care of him. This word-to-thing direction will become most important in later, more complex learning. The fact that a negative attitude toward school can be learned long before the child has any firsthand exposure to school is an illustration of the point. The acquisition of a vocabulary sensitizes the child to certain aspects of his environment, as we learned earlier in the discussion of perception.

The process of learning that things have names and the reverse is again accounted for in terms of a type of conditioned response in which the name and the thing are presented to the child simultaneously and in which eventually the name elicits in the child the same response that the object does whether or not the object is present. The name becomes a substitution for the thing.

However, this does not mean that when he hears the word the child has the same meaning in his mind as the adult does. More likely his referent for the word is much more diverse, or less precise, than that of the adult. In his very first usage of words, a single word is usually used as a sentence. It would probably be analyzed as a noun, but for the child it represents a complete thought. Thus, "bebe" will have to be interpreted by the adult in relation to the situation in which the word is spoken. It may mean "I, baby, want attention," or "There is another baby," or "Where is the other baby?" and so forth. The adult must be attuned to the accompanying gestures and the intonations used by the child if these word-sentences are to be understood.

At this point in the child's language development, words do not stand just for objects but also for situations or ways of handling situations. When the child uses the word "mama," it does not simply call up in his mind the image of his mother, but rather it is his way of dealing with the situation and says "I'm glad to see you because I know you and I like what you do for me."

We might say that at this stage the child is using speech instrumentally. He uses words as tools that enable him to obtain the responses he desires from his parents. He learns that a given word spoken in a given situation can lead to satisfying results. His use of language is only partially socialized. He recognizes some of the connection that the adult makes between the word and the object it symbolizes; but he uses the word in a much more flexible fashion, and in a variety of ways not used in adult speech, because he has not grasped its full public meaning.

The transition from the instrumental uses of sounds to the conventional use of speech seems to require one very important element—interaction with older members of society. At first, the *accompanying gestures* that go along with adult speech seem to be an important factor in enabling the child to attach conventional meanings to the words used. In addition, the *intonations* of the voice cannot be overlooked in helping the child understand adult speech. If you pick up a two-year-old and hold him gently in your arms and look into his eyes (accompanying gestures) and say in a soft and mellow voice (intonation), "You stinking, lousy pig," the gestures and voice intonation will far outweigh the conventional meanings of the words, even if he has had earlier experiences with those particular words. Of course, we try to keep intonation and gestures consistent with word meanings that we wish to convey to the child and thereby help him to gain understanding.

As the child grows and becomes more vocal, his speech and

grammar are continually corrected by the adults around him. Eventually he learns the conventional ways of putting words together and communicating through language.

As he moves along in this learning process he soon learns that words do not actually refer to single objects, but to classes of objects. The child accomplishes a rather amazing feat in learning a word like "dog." A two-year-old is held up before a dog and his mother says, "See the dog." The child may make an attempt at repeating the word "dog" and be corrected by the mother until he can say the word in a recognizable way. Later, other dogs come into the child's life. Each time, an adult repeats the word and relates it to the animal. Eventually, the child on seeing a four-legged animal with certain character- istics will say "dog," and it is discovered that he has learned the concept of dog. As he grows, he learns to discriminate between dogs and cats with considerable precision. Sometimes he makes a mistake and must be told that the funny-looking little animal is not really a cat, but a dog. The amazing part of this process is the child's ability to pick out from the examples that are presented to him the criteria that he will use later in discriminating between a dog and a cat. No one tells him to look at particular characteristics of the animal to make the discrimination. They simply say "That, that, and that are dogs and those over there are cats." It is entirely up to the child to pick out what factors are common to all dogs and are absent in all cats so that he can make this differentiation.

Learning the meaning of such concepts as money or race requires even more sophistication. A three-year-old is likely to equate money with shiny objects. Later he learns that these shiny objects have an exchange value. If he is allowed to have coins to play with and to take to the store with mother, he may learn that you can put the coins in a slot and receive a piece of candy or gum. Still later he will learn that money is used to get things from stores, although he may be confused when mother gives the man a piece of paper and gets money (coins) back as well as the groceries. But he is still a long way from knowing that money is earned, that people are not allowed to produce their own money, that money can be saved for later use, can be invested, or can be used to bribe people.

What our example makes clear is that the learning of language is a gradual ongoing process throughout childhood and throughout life. However, in the period between two and five years of age the child's vocabulary grows at a tremendous rate and during this period most children have developed the linguistic skills to the point that they are clearly engaging in what we have called conventional speech. They have developed the skills needed to meaningfully communicate with other human beings. Just as important, they have the ability to engage in mental activity—to think and to choose between alternative ways of responding. They have what some social psychologists call consciousness. In prelanguage stages of development, the child reacted in a spontaneous stimulus-response fashion to his encounters with his physical and social environment; now, with his linguistic skills, he has the power to delay the response, to contemplate the consequence of his act on others, and to respond only after he has considered a number of alternatives open to him. Consciousness flows from the ability to use symbols and thus to discriminate more specifically and exactly between stimuli.

From Egocentric to Relativistic Perspective

As the child's language skills increase, other changes are taking place. Of course, he is maturing physically and therefore has more freedom of movement. Soon he is not confined to a bed or crib but is crawling and, before long, walking. Both of these factors—increased language and locomotion—have an effect on his perception of the world about him. At first, the child is completely enclosed in his own perspectives and sees all things from within it. We describe his perception as *egocentric*. When an object is out of his sight, the child

assumes that it no longer exists. It is most difficult for him
during his first four or six years to learn to see the point of
view of other persons. A good example is the child's difficulty
with the terms such as "mother" and "brother." If asked, a five-
year-old will tell you if he has a brother, but he is confused
when asked how many brothers his brother has. Since he sees
the family only from his absolute perspective, he cannot see
the world from his brother's position. He knows that he has a
mother, but cannot understand that his mother could also have
a mother.

Rules required for cooperative behavior come only gradually, as he develops linguistic skills. At two, he may enjoy
playing in the sandbox in the company of other children his
age, but he does not play *with* them—claiming toys or teasing
but without coordinated play. Older children engage others in
group activity and seldom play alone, but this comes after they
have lost some of their egocentrism and are able to get outside
themselves.

Gradually, as the child's language increases and as he engages in more and more social relations, he begins to become
aware of the point of view of the people about him. He learns
that, from his brother's point of view, he is a brother and that
his mother must also have a mother of her own. He is beginning to think *relativistically*. It is impossible to specify an age
at which this transition starts or is completed. It is probably
true that at a given time a child may have developed a relativistic viewpoint in some areas, while in others he remains
egocentric. What is important is that eventually the egocen-
tricity disappears and the child can see the world from a
number of perspectives other than his own.

Development of Role-taking Skills

With the development of a relativistic perspective and with
the acquisition of linguistic skills to the point that the child
can engage in conscious mental activity, he can begin the

development of role-taking skills. Like the other processes described in this section, this one is gradual. It begins with the practice of young children imitating the roles of others in their play. At this period, the child actually plays the role of the others who are part of his social environment. He is the mailman, the grocer, or the mother. To enact these roles, he must have enough of the relative perspective to enable him to get some feeling from the way the others would act in their roles.

One of the most common instances of this type of role-playing takes place with dolls. This practice is particularly helpful for the child as he develops the foundations needed for role-taking. Remember that when we discussed role-taking, we emphasized that this process takes place in the person's imagination. He tries to put himself in the place of the other and look back at himself from the other's point of view, thus allowing him to anticipate the responses of others to the alternative actions that he is contemplating. Now, at this earlier stage in development, the child is actually playing at being the other person and in overt acts performs what he sees as their roles. The significance of the doll in this play is central in that it represents himself as an object. He is playing the role of his mother and in his play he also has a baby, so by acting out this role he is getting experience in taking the role of the mother and using her perspective in looking at him (at the time represented by the doll). This practice of role-playing in which he actually overtly plays the other's role is an important step and will lay the foundation for the time when he will take roles—that is, when in his imagination he will put himself in the place of the other.

This initial play and even the first role-taking is relatively simple and uncomplicated compared with what is to come. Here he is responding to only one person at a time. But as his circle of acquaintanceship is enlarged, as his own roles multiply in number, and as he becomes more proficient in his ability to communicate, the role-taking process becomes far more complicated.

Mead[2] has suggested that the child moves from the earlier play stage to what he calls a game stage. The child must learn to take the roles of the others in the situation, organize these roles into a coordinated whole, and be able to view his own behavior from this standpoint. Mead suggests that we contrast the play of the individual child with his involvement in an organized game. He uses the example of a baseball team. If an individual is to perform his role on a ball team, he must be able to put himself in the place of his teammates, not as individual players, but as a team. He must see them in relationship to each other—as a unit of organized roles—and even more important he must see his own role in relation to this organized unit.

This perception he has of the organized set of relationships is what Mead called the *generalized other*. As we have said in earlier chapters, the generalized other does not refer to the actual group of which the individual is a part, but rather it consists of his conception of the relationship between these roles and particularly their relationship to the role he is playing or anticipates playing in the group.

Development of the Self-concept

When the person has acquired linguistic skills, has developed a relative perspective, and has learned to engage in role-taking, he is beginning to get some notions about what he himself is like. In our earlier discussion of the self-concept, the dynamics that operate in the formation and change of the person's concept were explored. The child gains a conception of himself by role-taking—by putting himself in the place of the other and looking back upon himself as an object. He learns not only those attributes that might apply to him, such as are

[2] George Herbert Mead, *Mind, Self, and Society*, The University of Chicago Press, Chicago, 1934, pp. 149–164.

described by adjectives like "happy" or "active," but he also learns that certain role words refer to him ("boy," "five-year-old," and the like). Note the close link between language and self-conception. He is learning his role—that is, the behavior expected of him—by learning that certain labels apply to him. He is a happy, active, five-year-old boy.

As we mentioned in our earlier discussion, the conception that the individual develops of himself may prove somewhat misleading since his initial source of evidence is usually exclusively his parents. They are likely to have developed certain biases and may instill in him an unrealistic conception of his potentials. Most often this is rectified without too much pain by his peers or siblings as he gets out from his family and into a wider range of significant others.

The Content of Socialization—Roles, Norms, Values, and Attitudes

In some respects it can be said that much of what we have discussed in this chapter relates to the prerequisites for socialization. The development of language from simple sounds to the instrumental use of words and finally to conventional speech is a necessity in order for the individual to become a socialized member of society. The development of a relativistic perspective and the ability to take the role of the generalized other are also needed in order for socialization to take place. Remember that socialization itself is defined as the process whereby the individual learns the *habits, beliefs,* and *standards for behavior and judgment* that make him identifiable as a member of the group or society. The process presupposes language and a relativistic perspective. It is the process of interaction, in which, by role-taking and by being responsive to the devices of social control, the individual learns the roles he will be expected to play and can expect others to play, the norms that will govern his behavior, and the values he will place on actions and objects in his environment. A socialized child is more than a child that knows how to talk and take the perspective of the other. Before we will say that he is socialized, he must have used these skills in interacting with others long enough so that he has (1) learned just what are the norms that are pertinent to his role in the group, (2) developed the skills needed to fulfill these role requirements, and (3) internalized the motivation or desire to practice the behavior or hold the values required by the group. The purpose of socialization might be seen as providing the child with the knowledge, the ability, and the motivation to take on the behavior and values that make him identifiable as a member of the group or of the society.

It is valuable to direct our attention back to the earlier discussion of the primary group. Cooley felt that the primary group ought to be studied particularly because of its importance in the socialization process. He was emphasizing the point that a close, open relationship, in which some degree of intimacy was permissible and in which there existed emotional rather than pragmatic ties, was needed in order for the individual to become a socialized member of society. This should become clear in our present discussion, because we see how the individual must be able to perceive the responses and attitudes of those about him in order to pick up the norms, values, and attitudes that he must internalize in order to become socialized. Here, too, is where he receives the clearest picture of himself. Cooley's looking-glass self describes this process very well. He says that the person's conception of himself is the reflection of his behavior in the responses of his primary groups to him. He looks to the group as he would look into a mirror. Just as the mirror responds to his action by adjusting its image, so the group responds to his behavior by showing its approval or disapproval. In the primary group, he is most likely to see himself as others see him.

At first, this analysis of socialization might lead the student to wonder why, if the process works as described, we do not

all look and act more alike. Are we not suggesting that every-
one is forced to take on the norms and values of society?
Where does nonconformity come from? Are we not all
unique? The answers to these questions come in an analysis of
the socializing agencies and the diversity of encounters that
the individual has during his socialization period. First, the
society is not homogeneous in its values and norms, and there
is no absolute consensus as to the proper attitudes to be taken
toward various objects and activities. Then, of course, the
content of the socialization varies with the specific subcultural
values of the parents. Lower-class families set up quite different standards of expectations for their children than do middle-
class families. City residents have attitudes different from those
of rural dwellers, and so forth. Within the family, the content
of the socialization will vary depending upon the characteristics of the child and the expectations that are attached to these
characteristics. In middle-class American society, from the day
of birth a little girl is socialized differently than a little boy.
The girl is dressed in pink and the boy in blue. The girl soon is
wearing frilly dresses, and the baby boy must wear pants.
Toys differ; and, by school age, differentiation is extremely
clear-cut.

No two persons can possibly share the same socialization
experiences. Even identical twins are exposed to sufficiently
different aspects of the social and physical environment that
they develop a uniqueness of their own. This unique combination of roles, characteristics, and behavior pattern that becomes unique to the individual is what we generally call his
personality. However, the concept of personality implies more
than just the uniqueness of the individual. It implies that there
is a unity and consistency to the person as well as a uniqueness.
This tells us something more about socialization. The individual is responded to by others as a unity, with the expectation that there will be a consistency among the different roles
and attitudes he is expected to take. For example, if he has

been socialized to strive for intellectual achievement and his behavior reflects this value, we would also expect him to have a positive admiration for others who have accomplished the stature he himself is striving for. That is, we would expect that the various dimensions of his personality would fit together into some meaningful whole. This was also reflected in an earlier chapter when we talked about his self-concept being the *organization* of qualities that he attributes to himself. Based on this, his behavior may be regarded at least in part as an effort to maintain his unity and integrity.

SOCIALIZATION AFTER CHILDHOOD

At one time the concept of socialization was used almost exclusively to refer to the process in childhood considered in the preceding section. However, it is apparent that many of the same processes are involved when adults move to new groups or take on new positions. The application of the conception of socialization to adulthood has proved very useful in explaining the behavior of individuals at these points of transition in their lives.

Socialization as a Lifetime Process

It is possible to think of socialization as a continuous process that begins at birth and ends at death. Here we would be taking the position that socialization does not end when the child has developed the factors discussed earlier in this chapter but rather continues as he moves from one setting to another. As can be seen from Figure 6, the typical person finds himself in many different positions that are related to his age, and he must learn the roles and values that are attached to these various positions as he moves from one to the other. That is, he must become socialized into each new position.

The movement from childhood through adolescence to adulthood is a particularly interesting transition. Some have

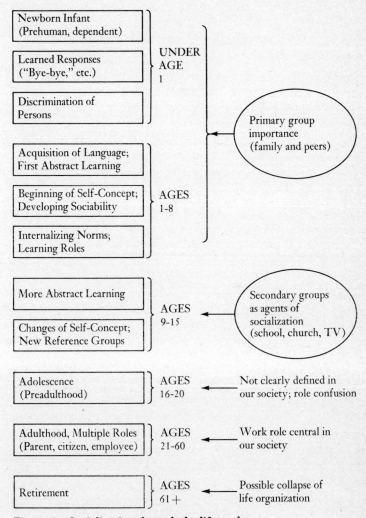

Figure 6   Socialization through the life cycle.

attributed the behavior of the adolescent to biological changes that take place during this period. Certainly these changes are taking place, but to suggest that the restlessness, confusion, and rebelliousness of many adolescents is due to the biological changes within the body may be quite misleading. Anthropologists tell us that in other cultures no such behavioral attributes are seen in young persons of this age. What might better account for these characteristics is the poor job we do of socializing children during this period of their lives. Remember that the socialized person must have directed toward him a consistent pattern of expectations that he can use as a source of evidence to determine his conception of himself and the expectations for his behavior. In adolescence these expectations are likely to be considerably less than clear and consistent. In some ways, the adolescent is like the foreman discussed earlier under role-conflict. Different sectors of his social environment are placing inconsistent demands upon him. Sometimes he is expected to act like an adult, at other times like a child. Moreover, the very socializing agency that he has relied upon for so long, his family, is likely to be the most inconsistent of all. He is told to grow up and act like an adult. When he appears to be lazy, he is punished for his childlike behavior. The father says to the fourteen-year-old, "You're an adult now, go out and earn some money, pay for some of your own clothes, and earn the respect of us adults." The boy looks around to determine how adults act so he can use them as models in order to behave as his father wishes. He observes his parents; he watches adults on television and listens to his peers talk about the adults they know. What do adults do that is different from what children do? He sees adults with a lot more freedom. They drink liquor freely and frequently. They engage in sexual activity. They drive big and fast cars. So he decides that he will act like an adult. This, for him, could mean getting drunk, racing the family car, and ending up in the back seat of the car with his girl friend. When his father finds out about some or all of this behavior, he becomes furious. He informs his son that he is not old enough to drink and drive like that and that the activity in the back seat of the car is reserved for an older age. He finds that when the label "adult" is applied to the adolescent it holds a different set of role expectations than it does when applied to older persons. Thus, adolescence is a period of social confusion.

The next important transition is from the position of student to the position of worker, from the trainee to the employee. This is usually somewhat easier than the change discussed above, because there is usually some preparation for the change in high school or college; and the individual has more of an idea about what is expected of him. But of far greater importance is what we might call the social visibility of the change. The adolescent, reflecting the confusion of those about him, is never certain whether he is a child or an adult. But when the young person finishes school and starts on his first job, there is no such confusion. This does not mean that the transition has no ambiguities, only that they are less severe than in the earlier case. In any change of roles, there is a period of uncertainty when the person is learning the norms and values of the new position. It is not unusual for the new employee to go through a period of informal testing by the older workers to see if he can live up to their expectations. As in most changes, this initial period will have its uncomfortable moments until the expectations are learned.

Formerly in our society, once the person had made his transition into the position of employee or the woman had moved into her position of housewife and mother, the positions remained relatively stable for a long time. Of course, there were promotions and the wife had more children or the children got married and moved away, but these were all part of the organization of things and were not seen as abrupt changes. However, more recently, with the dramatic and rapid technological and social changes taking place in our society, it is not unusual for a person to change his career three or four times during his lifetime—not just a change in his job, but a complete change in his career. The woman who works is likely to find it necessary to change even more. These are the types of changes that require resocialization. Thus, socialization is a more continuous phenomenon than one might expect.

Additionally, the changes in our technology in the area of health and medicine have led to another significant area of socialization—the transition between the employee position and that of retirement. More and more persons are living for a longer time after they retire. This is particularly interesting to the social psychologist studying socialization, because in many ways retirement is a new position. Fifty years ago, the relatively few persons who lived for any time after retirement could be taken care of with little concern, and if they were mistreated their numbers were so small that little attention was given them. Now with the large number of retired persons, we have a new position. Retirement homes and villages have sprung up to accommodate these older persons and in many ways to define for them what their new role *should* be. But even here the problems have not been resolved, and it is generally agreed that we do not treat our aged with the concern that we have for other groups within the society.

Orville Brim, Jr.,[3] suggests that there are changes in the content of socialization that make adult socialization significantly different from that which takes place in childhood. Most important, he feels, is the change to a concern that deals primarily with knowledge of overt behavioral demands in roles and little concern with influences on motivations of a fundamental kind. Note that in adult socialization any change in basic values or motivations requires the rejection of values that the individual already holds, whereas in childhood the

---

[3] Orville G. Brim, Jr., and Stanton Wheeler, *Socialization after Childhood*, John Wiley & Sons, Inc., New York, 1966, pp. 1–46.

problem was to develop these motivations and values where none existed. This can be demonstrated in the case of the person who finds himself technologically unemployed. Society will not try to change his basic values, which say that he should be financially responsible for his family and should find productive employment. Rather the socialization process will be directed at changing his knowledge and abilities so that he can find useful employment. His values and motivations are changed only on a superficial level, but his basic values learned in childhood remain unchanged. His knowledge and ability to perform behavioral tasks are likely to have changed considerably.

During the early period of socialization, a great deal of time and effort is put into acquiring new material, developing vocabulary, learning role-expectations, and the like. Later in the life cycle, the objective of socialization is more toward directing the individual to put together the various materials learned in early socialization and to apply them to new forms of responses. When one goes to college, reading, writing, and arithmetic are no longer taught, but the individual is expected to learn to use these acquired skills to deal with more complex responses to the demands that are placed upon him. Brim[4] suggests that as a person moves through the life cycle another change in the content of socialization is "from the acquisition of new material to the synthesis of the old."

Other changes that take place in the content of socialization are changes from a concern with idealism to a concern with realism; from learning expectations, to learning how to handle conflicts among expectations; increased exposure to secondary, rather than primary relationships; and a move from concern with instilling general societal demands to a concern with more specific requirements for particular roles. Each of these changes that we have mentioned is not absolute in the sense

[4] *Ibid.*, p. 28.

that the change is never complete. Certainly, adults still learn
new material and may on occasion be pressured to change
some rather basic values. What we are saying is that adult
socialization uses childhood socialization as a foundation and
comes at a time when, for the most part, biological maturity
has occurred and can no longer be a limiting factor. Therefore, the emphasis on the content of adult socialization changes
and it becomes more an agency for the adjustment of the
individual to the demands placed upon him in his adult role in
society.

Group Socialization

Not all changes that confront the individual in society are
directly related to his life cycle. He may join a new group
either voluntarily (such as a bowling team or a political club)
or involuntarily (when he is drafted or sent to prison). The
process of socialization into these new groups is much like the
socialization into society. As in the case of adult socialization
within the life cycle, the group does not need to start from the
beginning in socializing the individual. He has learned much
about the group before he joins. Even in the involuntary situation, it is unusual for a new member to join the group with no
expectation as to what will be required of him. When the
person aspired to become a member of the group, he may have
used that group as a reference group long before he is actually
accepted as a member and therefore may have patterned his
behavior after the expectations that he sees as the standards
that the group holds.

During the entry into the new group, the individual is likely
to go through a stage in which he finds himself quite uncomfortable. He must be particularly sensitive to the responses of
others so that he may learn what is expected of him before he
violates any serious norm of the group. We might say that
during this period the individual overconforms. That is, he
adheres so strictly to what he sees as the norms of the group
that he stands out for his conformity. It takes a longer period

of socialization for him to learn just what are the tolerance limits for the norms. He must learn the subtle "exceptions to the rule" and the patterns of enforcement before he is a completely socialized member of the group.

In the involuntary groups, the individual may resist full and complete socialization. In prison, he may not want to take on the values of his fellow inmates, but it does not take him long to learn that it is a good idea to at least learn the norms for his behavior so that he can act as if he is conforming even though he has not accepted the value system of the inmate community.

SUMMARY

In order for the individual to emerge as a socialized adult member of society, three requirements must be met. First, he must have a physiological mechanism of great complexity and without serious neurological or glandular defects. Second, he must be a member of a coherent and functioning society. Third, he must have a long history of apprenticeship in primary groups. In this chapter, we have seen how these three factors work together to enable the individual to learn the language and perspectives needed to later take on the norms, values, and attitudes that make him recognizable as a member of society. He learns the expectations of society, the skills needed to fulfill these expectations in the particular roles that he enacts, and finally the motivation that leads him to desire to conform to these expectations of the group or society. This involves the development of role-taking ability and a coherent conception of self.

Socialization continues throughout the life cycle. However, as the individual moves beyond childhood, the content of socialization changes, with more emphasis placed on specific adjustments to changing situations than on the learning of new material or the internalization of basic values or motives. The process of socialization into a group is much like the processes that are involved in socialization in the society after childhood.

SUGGESTED REFERENCES

* Brim, Orville G., and Stanton Wheeler: *Socialization after Child-hood*, John Wiley & Sons, Inc., New York, 1966.
Two studies of the process of socialization as it operates throughout the life cycle.

* Clausen, John A. (ed.): *Socialization and Society*, Little, Brown and Company, Boston, 1968.
Seven excellent papers on various aspects of socialization.

* Coser, Rose Laub (ed.): *Life Cycle and Achievement in America*, Harper & Row, Publishers, New York, 1969 (Harper Torch-books).
Nine articles with topics ranging from childhood to death, all regarding the consequence of American society on various aspects of the life cycle.

* Elkin, Frederick: *The Child and Society*, Random House, Inc., New York, 1960.
A short statement of socialization from the viewpoint of a sociologist.

* Erikson, Erik H.: *Childhood and Society*, 2d ed., W. W. Norton & Company, Inc., New York, 1963.
A psychoanalytic view of the process of socialization.

* Friedenberg, Edgar Z.: *The Vanishing Adolescent*, Dell Publishing Co., Inc., New York, 1959.

* _____: *Coming of Age in America*, Random House, Inc., New York, 1965 (Vintage Books).
Two books by Friedenberg describe the effects of adult behavior (apathy, indifference, and the like) on the adolescent in American society.

* Goodman, Paul: *Growing up Absurd*, Random House, Inc., New York, 1960.
A popular book on the problems of youth growing up in a highly organized society.

* Piaget, Jean: *The Language and Thought of the Child*, World Publishing Company, New York, 1955 (Meridian Books).
The famous Swiss psychologist's classic analysis of language development in children. There are several other books by Piaget on early child development.

* Roszak, Theodore: *The Making of a Counter Culture*, Doubleday & Company, Inc., Garden City, N.Y., 1969 (Anchor Books).
Reflections on the technocratic society and its youthful opposition.

* Sebald, Hans: *Adolescence: A Sociological Analysis*, Appleton-Century-Crofts, New York, 1968.
A thorough analysis of the topic of adolescence and the problems of youth within society.

* Spitzer, Stephan P.: *The Sociology of Personality*, Van Nostrand Reinhold Company, New York, 1969.
Readings on personality development as a system of self-other relationships.

* References marked with asterisk are available in paperback.

NINE

COLLECTIVE BEHAVIOR
AND MASS COMMUNICATION

This chapter deals with the social influence of nongroup collectives with
which the individual is confronted. *Collective behavior* is a term used to refer to
*a class of social behavior that is relatively
uninfluenced by cultural norms or customs.* It usually is seen as taking the form
of *crowds, mobs, panics, and crazes. Mass
communication,* which is quite another
phenomenon, concerns *the exposure of a
large, dispersed, and heterogeneous audience to messages transmitted by an impersonal source for whom the audience is
anonymous.* These two different phenomena are considered together in the same
chapter because they both represent
situations in which the individual's behavior is influenced by a source that is
clearly social in nature but does not fit
our understanding of the group and cannot be explained in terms of the dynamics
we have discussed under that topic. Up
to this point, we have been interested in
how the individual is socialized into
society and how his behavior is motivated
and constrained by what he sees as the
norms of the group and the expectations
that the group members have for him.

We have seen how he puts himself in the place of the other and looks back at himself and in his imagination considers alternatives for his actions. We placed importance on the presence of the other and how the other's reaction or response to the individual was crucial in determining for the individual what he sees as himself and what he feels are the expectations of others. The importance of the primary group, in which the individual learns to conform because of his emotional commitment to the members, and the tendency of the individual to perform a role as an incumbent were seen as essential to the understanding of man's behavior in groups. But these are not the only ways in which men are influenced by other men and by society. In this chapter we will deal with two other ways—collective behavior and mass communication.

THE CROWD

There is no precise definition of collective behavior that satisfactorily delimits all the forms of social behavior that have been studied under this heading. As well as those forms listed above, others have included everything from fads to revolutions. To avoid being bogged down on a question of definition, we will simply take a single form of collective behavior and consider it as an example of ways in which the individual can be influenced by others outside the group. For this purpose we have chosen the crowd.

The crowd has been of interest to sociologists since before the turn of the century. More recently, social psychologists have turned their attention to the study of the crowd as an interesting source of information about group emotions. The crowd is characterized by its short-lived existence, the close physical contact of the members with each other, and the lack of organization and structure, which leads to spontaneous, rather than calculated, interaction. Our decision to consider the crowd a nongroup is somewhat arbitrary, since interaction, norms, and roles are not missing in the crowd but these elements exist to a much lesser extent than they do in the type of groups talked about earlier, and they play a relatively insignificant role in determining the behavior observed in the crowd as compared with their effects in groups. For this reason, some have described crowds as groups in the process of organizing.

There are many different types of crowds. Herbert Blumer[1] identifies several different types starting with the simplest of aggregates, which he calls the *casual crowd*. Exemplified by persons waiting for a street car, the casual crowd is characterized by its momentary existence, its loose organization, and its lack of unity. Note, however, that it is not completely without those characteristics that go into the analysis of a group. There is some interaction in that persons coordinate their activity in getting onto the bus. They bring with them some role differentiation and may let the old lady enter the bus before the young men. There are some norms for behavior inasmuch as they all stand and treat each other with silent respect. But compared with groups like the family, a gang, or the members of your class in social psychology, this casual crowd has much less of the ingredients that define a group.

The next type of crowd Blumer calls the *conventionalized crowd*. Much like the casual crowd, the conventionalized crowd could be illustrated by the spectators at a ball game. Here there are expressed or conventionalized ways of acting. These regularized ways of behaving, established frequently through years of tradition, make the conventionalized crowd distinct from the casual crowd and account for the behavior of the participants in the crowd.

The most interesting of the crowds that Blumer discusses is the *acting crowd*. Since this type of crowd best exemplifies

---

[1] Herbert Blumer, "Collective Behavior," in Alfred McCung Lee (ed.), *The Principles of Sociology*, Barnes & Noble, Inc., New York, 1951, pp. 167–223. The discussion that follows is heavily influenced by Blumer's material.

what interests us in this text, we shall limit our further discussion to this category of crowd.

THE ACTING CROWD

As compared with other types of crowds, the acting crowd has the added feature of action directed toward a goal. The activity and energy of the crowd are directed toward an objective or aim. It has been possible to delimit some of the steps in the formation of the acting crowd, and these seem to form an excellent foundation for our understanding of the crowd effect on the individual.

The first step is the occurrence of some type of *exciting event* that focuses the attention of the individuals who are together and arouses their interest. When the individual responds by becoming preoccupied with this event, he may already be on the way to losing some of his ordinary self-control. This excitement from arousing impulses and emotions puts the individual in a state of tension and prepares him to move into action. But the individual is not alone. A number of people are stimulated by the same exciting event; and this fact leads quickly to the second step in the formation of the acting crowd—the beginning of the *milling process*, which takes the form of the circulation of the people within the crowd. The preoccupation with the exciting event has led them to lose some of their normal inhibitions, and they find it easy to exchange comments and opinions with strangers toward whom they would ordinarily be more reserved. This physical closeness to others, the individual's awareness of the common mood of excitement, and the general moving about adds greatly to the excitement. The feelings of each are conveyed to the others; thus the milling process leads to a common mood of intense excitement, with the individuals in the crowd developing a sense of cohesion or rapport. With this feeling of excitement and rapport, each individual tends to become highly sensitive and susceptible to the moods and feeling of the others.

The next stage in the formation of the acting crowd is the *emergence of a common object of attention* on which the excitement, impulses, and feelings of the people become focused. This common object is frequently the same exciting event that caught their attention in the first place, but it could be another image created by or during the milling process. This object gives a common orientation to the crowd members and so provides a common objective for their activity.

The last step occurs when the individuals direct their aroused impulses and excitement toward the common objective and *act* with unity and purpose. At this point, a leader may emerge to direct the specific behavior that is aimed at the goal. The aggressive manner in which the crowd attacks this emergent objective is typical of the acting crowd. Here we use the word "aggressive" to connote active, vigorous behavior, not necessarily hostile in nature.

The four steps might be summarized as (1) the attention-focusing exciting event, (2) milling, (3) emergence of a common objective, and (4) aggressive action toward the objective.

Consider the following example: You are at an exciting football game that ends on a disputed play in which the opposing team scores a field goal and wins the game. Up to this point, you were part of what we have described as a conventionalized crowd; but now, with the occurrence of this exciting event, the scene is ripe for the emergence of an acting crowd. You have been excited by the close ending to the game, you can feel the adrenalin increasing the tension within you, and you feel the need for action. Before you really consider it (you are losing some of your ordinary self-control) you find yourself joining the "flood" of persons drifting from the stands onto the playing field. There you walk about talking excitedly to persons you have never seen before, telling how you saw the field goal miss. This milling intensifies your excitement and makes you feel united with these strangers about you.

Suddenly someone yells, "Let's get the goal posts!" Before you know it, the attention of the entire crowd is directed toward the common objective of tearing down the goal posts. You join in the chant: "We want the goal posts!" You help the others in pulling down the posts and end up fighting in the mud for a piece of them for yourself.

The four steps can be easily identified in the above example. The whole event may not have taken more than half an hour. The exciting end to the game, the milling, the emergence of the goal posts as a common objective, and the aggressive action taken toward this objective were all done before you knew what happened. You went through this action without the aid of the critical type of role-taking we have described in earlier chapters, which you would ordinarily use in calmer settings. You were not considering in your mind what the responses of others would be to a number of alternative actions you might take in these situations. Rather, you were acting on the basis of aroused impulses, feelings, and imagery.

From our analysis so far, we can point out some of the characteristics of the crowd that make it essentially different from the group. First, it has *no heritage*, no accumulation of tradition that might be used to guide the activity of the persons involved. There are few rules or expectations to govern the behavior of the individuals, and such conventions as do exist either emerge from the short existence of the crowd or consist of strong moral tendencies that overrule the spontaneous impulses that have been aroused. In the last instance, the moral grounds are likely to be strictly individualistic and could not be described as crowd norms. We see that there is very little of what we have described as essential to the group. There is little social organization, division of labor, or role differentiation. There are no consistent set of norms and no moral conscience. If a leader does emerge, his influence is likely to be sporadic and inconsistent.

The second characteristic of the crowd is the basis for its action. In the crowd, the individuals are acting on the basis of *aroused impulses*. Group members operate on the basis of rational, considered forethought, but the crowd acts on the basis of spontaneity and irrationality. It is little wonder that crowd behavior has been described as strange, forbidding, fickle, and irresponsible.

This can be better understood when we consider some of the characteristics of the individuals in the crowd. They have *lost* the ordinary *critical understanding* and judgment as a result of being caught up in the collective excitement that dominates their actions. Their attention is so drawn toward the objectives of the crowd that they sometimes lose all self-concern. As if in a hypnotic state, they respond immediately to the suggestions and actions of others without first subjecting these gestures of others to their own critical judgment. This *suggestibility* of the members of the crowd to the actions or remarks of others is an important factor in accounting for the aggressive and frequently asocial nature of the action of the crowd.

Early in our discussion of groups, we suggested that a group might be conceived of as men acting together as a unit. Correspondingly, we can think of a crowd as men responding to a common contagion. Note that the acting crowd exists only during those periods when the action is taking place, and this occurs only when certain conditions are present. For example, most persons can recall sometime in their lives when they were exposed to the first two stages in the development of the acting crowd. Perhaps you stopped to observe a fire. You were drawn by the excitement of this event, the red lights, the sirens, and so forth. Next you found that there were others like you who were milling around the scene, telling their version of what had happened or what they expected to happen. You felt the loss of self-concern, the excitement, and the lack of ordinary inhibitions; however, chances were that no common object of attention emerged toward which these impulses and feelings could be directed. The potential was there, and were the fire chief to suggest to the crowd that they could help clear the furniture out of the house you probably would have joined in and done your part—forgetting your bad back, your appointment for that hour, and the fact that you were wearing your best suit. This example should be a reminder that all crowd action is not necessarily negative or undesirable. Many heroic and superhuman feats have been accomplished when individuals were caught up in the spell of the crowd. What is central is that the action is emotional, spontaneous, and without critical deliberation.

In some situations, the likelihood of the emergence of an acting crowd is greatly increased by the social conditions of the community or society. This was clearly demonstrated in the report of the President's Commission on Civil Disorders (better known as the Kerner Commission's riot report).[2] The following excerpts are taken directly from the portion of their report that discusses "the riot process." We present it here to show how social conditions can create the state of unrest and tension that can lead directly to active aggressive crowd behavior, in this case rioting. In the summer of 1967, the Negro communities in many of the major cities of the United States were scenes of rioting of various degrees of intensity. This is the way the commission described the riot process:

> The Commission has found no "typical" disorder in 1967 in terms of intensity of violence and extensiveness of damage. To determine whether, as is sometimes suggested, there was a typical "riot process," we examined 24 disorders which occurred during 1967 in 20 cities and three university settings. We have concentrated on four aspects of that process:

[2] National Advisory Commission on Civil Disorders, *Report* (The Kerner Report), Bantam Books, Inc., New York, 1968.

- The accumulating reservoir of grievances in the Negro community;
- "Precipitating" incidents and their relationship to the reservoir of grievances;
- The development of violence after its initial outbreak;
- The control effort, including official force, negotiation, and persuasion.

We found a common social process operating in all 24 disorders in certain critical respects. These events developed similarly, over a period of time and out of an accumulation of grievances and increasing tension in the Negro community. Almost invariably, they exploded in ways related to the local community and its particular problems and conflicts. . . .

The specific content of the expressed grievances varied somewhat from city to city. But in general, grievances among Negroes in all the cities related to prejudice, discrimination, severely disadvantaged living conditions and a general sense of frustration about their inability to change those conditions. . . .

Grievances about police practices, unemployment and underemployment, housing and other objective conditions in the ghetto were aggravated in the minds of many Negroes by the inaction of municipal authorities. . . .

In virtually every case a single "triggering" or "precipitating" incident can be identified as having immediately preceded—within a few hours and in generally the same location—the outbreak of disorder. But this incident was usually relatively minor, even trivial, by itself. . . .

We found that violence was generated by an increasingly disturbed social atmosphere, in which typically not one, but a series of incidents occurred over a period of weeks or months. . . .

As we see it, the prior incidents and the reservoir of underlying grievances contributed to a cumulative process of mounting tension that spilled over into violence when the final incident occurred.[3]

The commission's report of the incident leading up to the first day of violence in Newark, New Jersey, provides a more

[3] *Ibid.*, pp. 116–118.

specific example of what was happening throughout the country. In Newark, before the day of the violence, there had been in the Negro community a number of incidents involving the police and their relations with the community. On July 12, 1967, at approximately 9:30 P.M., the following took place:

> A Negro cab driver was injured during or after a traffic arrest in the heart of the Central Ward. Word spread quickly and a crowd gathered in front of the Fourth Precinct station-house across the street from a large public housing project. [At 11:30 P.M.] The crowd continued to grow until it reached 300 to 500 people. One or two Molotov cocktails were thrown at the station-house. Shortly after midnight the police dispersed the crowd, and the window-breaking and looting began a few minutes later. By about 1:00 A.M., the peak level of violence for the first night was reached.[4]

It should be possible for us to apply our analysis of crowd behavior, discussed earlier in this section, to the understanding of what went on in these riots. First, we need to recognize that the individuals involved lived under conditions that made them quite susceptible to these types of reactions.

Let us consider one hypothetical person who might have been involved in one of these riots. He was a black male, age twenty-four. He had looked for a job earlier in the summer, but after several rejections had given up to spend most of his time sitting around the house, sometimes taking care of the baby while his wife went out to deliver the ironing that she did to support her family. It is hot in Newark in the summer (as it is in Detroit, Washington, Cincinnati, and most of the other cities where riots occurred in 1967). On July 12, the heat was getting to the baby, and it cried most of the day. The three-year-old son and five-year-old daughter were around the house all day, since the schools were out for the summer. There was no day-care center and the playgrounds of

[4] *Ibid.*, p. 119.

the city were not located in the ghetto where the family lived. The kids were cross and fussy because there was not enough to eat. When the wife returned home, she was tired and complained that she had to prepare dinner after her hard day's work. Finally, after smelling the greasy food being cooked and listening to the complaints and almost overcome by the heat, the young man grabbed the last can of beer from the refrigerator and left the house. Outside it was only slightly cooler, but the fresh air and the beer helped his disposition somewhat. He was hungry, but could not face up to going back into the house to eat his dinner. He noted that several of his neighbors had also come out and were sitting on their stoops, many drinking beer or wine. He joined them and they talked about how the week before several of the Newark police had helped the East Orange police in a run-in with a group of Negro men in East Orange. Soon they were exchanging stories of police brutality. After an hour or so of this, they heard a commotion down at the end of the block and decided to walk down to see what was going on. They came upon a crowd of persons standing across from the station-house. People excitedly came up to them and told them of a black cab driver who had been severely beaten by the police, arrested, and taken into the station. As our young man moved through the milling crowd, he heard various versions of the incident and repeated his understanding of it to newcomers as they joined the crowd. As the crowd grew so did the excitement. The appearance of police officers at about midnight caused our young man and those about him to let out shouts and catcalls, but when the police appeared to turn towards them they impulsively turned and ran down the street. By now he was in a wild state of tension. He had forgotten about the hunger and the heat that had bothered him earlier. Now he was completely caught up in the physical activity around him and the impulses that had been aroused within him. The frustrations of the day and of his whole life seemed to have come to the surface. When the person next to him picked up a rock and hurled it through a store window, he was quick to follow. The sound of breaking glass and the shouting of the crowd only added to the excitement. He was ready to follow the slightest suggestion. Before the night was over he had broken many windows and had set fire to a building, and he came home with an armload of looted merchandise.

Our example, although hypothetical, is not an exaggeration of the actions and feelings of many of the rioters. In some ways, we could say that Negro communities in almost all large cities in that summer of 1967 were in a perpetual state of tension and were simply waiting for the precipitating incident to lead them into aggressive crowd behavior.

We have tried to show in this section how it is possible for an individual's behavior to be determined or influenced by the social conditions under which he is expected to live—the prejudice, the oppression, and the physical environment—and later to be affected by the mutual contagion of the crowd he joins. He is not playing a role or considering the expectations of society or even of his own subculture. He is allowing the suggestions of the crowd to determine how he will act out the frustrations that have surfaced.

MASS COMMUNICATION

In this chapter, we are discussing social influences that do not fit the definition and analysis of the group. In the first section, we used as an example the crowd; and we saw how emotional excitement, close proximity of others, and related conditions profoundly affected the behavior of individuals in the crowd. In this section, we shall discuss mass communication—a situation in which the source of influence appears to be impersonal and remote.

We defined mass communication earlier in the chapter as the exposure of a large, dispersed, and heterogeneous audience to messages transmitted by impersonal sources for whom the audience is anonymous. To relate this to our original discussion of communication in Chapter 4, it can be seen that the source of the message in mass communication differs from face-to-face communication in that the person is replaced with a communication organization such as a newspaper, broadcasting network, or publishing house. The destinations toward which the message is directed are individuals who are exposed to the media in one way or the other. They are likely to be unknown to the source and are not available for direct feedback. In the face-to-face situation, the source looks to the destination for a nod of the head or other response that will give him a hint of the effectiveness of his message, but there is no such link in mass communication. What little feedback there is usually comes after the original communication has been completed, and it can be used only to revise future messages, not to improve ongoing ones. For example, if newspaper advertisement of a product is followed by a decline in the sales of that product, this change in consumer behavior may serve as feedback from the ad, informing the communication organization that the intended message is not getting across to the destination.

In American society, the most important mass media are television, radio, newspapers, magazines, and books. Although there is great variation within and among these various media, they all share the distinction of being remote from their intended destination, and their audiences can be thought of as relatively isolated individuals. A person reads, listens to, or watches the media pretty much by himself. He does not know if his neighbor is listening to the same program; and, when he sits down to read the comic strip, he is not likely to feel much kinship with or group feeling for all the others who are reading the same strip.

Why should we as social psychologists be interested in mass communication? To answer this question, we must be aware of some of the functions of mass communication in our society. Although there are many functions, the following four are probably central to our concern: to inform, to entertain, to influence, and to sell. This last function may be particularly characteristic of the mass media within the United States since most channels of the mass media are operated as private business enterprises. The central goal is the pursuit of commercial gain. Almost all of our television and radio stations broadcast many commercials, and our newspapers and magazines are heavy with ads. This is significant for our concern since every commercial or advertisement is an attempt to influence the behavior or attitudes of the individuals reading or listening. They are attempts to make you want to buy their product or vote for their candidate.

The information function of the mass media, which is most conventionally provided by way of the "news," can be seen as central and vital to the existence of a complex society such as ours. Lasswell[5] has expanded on this simple notion of information by suggesting that the information performs three functions crucial to the operation of society. First, it functions as a *surveillance* of the environment, disclosing threats and opportunities that might lead to changes in the status positions between or within the community or society. Second, it coordinates the component parts of society in making a response to the environment. Finally, the information function of the mass media leads to the transmission of the social heritage from one generation to the next.

Radio and television devote most of their time to what we have labeled entertainment. Music, ball games, movies, talk shows, and westerns are all examples of the use of the media to entertain. Of course, these programs also help to transmit the social heritage, but their primary purpose seems to be to enter-

[5] Harold D. Lasswell, "The Structure and Function of Communication," in Lyman Bryson (ed.), *The Communication of Ideas,* Harper & Row, Publishers, New York, 1948.

tain the audience, or at least to provide them with something that is attractive enough to keep them tuned to that channel. Of course, these entertaining programs are brought to you, not as a public service by their sponsors, but to provide those sponsors with a means of getting your attention so that they may present to you their products with the hope that you will then go out and purchase them. This is not to say that the audience is being duped into listening to commercials, but rather that the sophisticated audiences of today agree that in exchange for the entertainment they will tolerate interruptions for commercials.

Other functions of the mass media are not so obvious. The media, sometimes intentionally, but often unintentionally, have the function of providing models for behavior. In some instances, propaganda is used in a deliberate attempt to influence values and beliefs. In other instances, the content of the ads and entertainment functions to convey particular norms of society. Some suggest that the media provide models for behavior, which are copied, particularly by the young. The portrayal of violence, crime, and sex on television, in magazines, and in books (particularly comic books for children) has come under attack by several sources concerned with the effects that the media will have on the behavior of the members of society. We shall discuss the effects of the media below.

Although we cannot be certain just what effect the exposure to the media is having on the individual, we do have some impressive statistics on mass media consumption. We are told that children by the age of ten are spending more time in front of the television set than they spend in school; every day millions and millions of American housewives watch or listen to so-called soap operas. With this vast amount of exposure of the American public, it would seem important for the social psychologist to learn what he can about the effect that this experience is having.

You will recall that we began this section by stating that we were interested in the influences that affected the behavior of individuals in society. We saw how this occurred in the crowd. Now we have before us quite a different situation. What is the effect on the behavior of an individual of his exposure to an impersonal communication network that has as one of its explicit functions the influencing of his behavior? In terms of the consumption of time, many children in American society by the age of five are spending more time in front of the television set than they spend with their families. Does television substitute as a socializing agency? We do not have as clear answers to these questions as we would like, but we do have some hints that are worth considering.

Perhaps the most valuable finding of the studies on the effect of mass communication is that the mass referred to is not the isolated, heterogeneous collection of independent individuals that the word implies—at least not in terms of the actual effect that the media are having. It is true that the individual may be exposed to the media when he is by himself, but his interpretation, evaluation, and eventually his response to the media are very likely to be a consequence of his involvement in small groups. In the many studies of the relative effect of personal face-to-face influence as compared with the influence of the mass media, the data always show the personal influence to be more effective. This is quite consistent with what we have considered earlier in connection with primary and secondary relationships. The primary relationship is almost always the more influential of the two. However, this does not mean that the mass media are not effective. There is a *two-step flow of communication*, in which ideas flow from the media to the "opinion leader" to the members of his group.[6] Some individuals have a great deal more exposure to the media than others. They watch television more, they read more of the

6 Elihu Katz and Paul F. Lazarsfeld, *Personal Influence*, The Free Press, New York, 1964.

newspaper, and they listen to the radio more often. These persons become the experts in the group on what is going on in the world. Opinion leaders in most groups tend to specialize in the sense that one person would be looked to for an appraisal of a televised ball game, another for an evaluation of the world news, and a third for information on the best dishwasher to buy.

In addition to the influence of the opinion leader in selecting, interpreting, and evaluating the media, the group itself functions to affect the consequences of the mass media. Perhaps the greatest effects of the media are derived by feeding ideas and information into small groups wherein the actual effects are determined. In some groups, it is a sign of status to be familiar with some content of the mass media. The teenager must be up on the latest hits and the businessman is expected to have read his copy of the *Wall Street Journal*. It is not unusual for the members of a group to expect that all the other members have read the morning newspaper so that their coffee break can be spent reinterpreting the stories of the day. Each individual brings his interpretation into the group. Some interpretations will be listened to more than others, but in the end every individual in the group is likely to come out with an understanding different from the one he started with. So the influence of mass communication is not as much a direct influence as it is a secondary influence, reflected to the group and back again.

There has been a great deal of concern about how the mass media affect voting behavior. Of course, in a mass society such as ours, in which the people are called upon to make political decisions by voting, the media are essential in getting information about the candidates to the electorate. Again, the two-step flow of communication seems to work for many persons. That is, those in a given group who read magazine articles and listen to speeches come to the group as experts on the various candidates. These individuals are more influential in determining the group member's evaluations of the candidate than are firsthand exposures to information through the mass media. If there is no dominant opinion leader in the group, the members of the group probably each contribute bits and pieces and together they work out an evaluation. Of course, this is a subtle process, with some persons' evaluations and comments carrying more weight than those of others. Also, the group does not end its discussion by saying, "O.K., we're all agreed to vote for Joe Smith." Rather, the discussion ends after the various opinions have been expressed, countered, and interpreted. Sometimes, it is not until later that the individual puts together the new information and interpretations that he has learned from his group experience and actually experiences a change in opinion. This is called the sleeper effect.

It seems fair to conclude that mass communication performs a very important function in the socialization of the members of society. We can only speculate about its effect in the early years of the child's development, before he has much peer contact outside the home. When the television set is used as a baby-sitter and reduces the interaction between parent and child, it undoubtedly has some effect on that relationship. During the early school years, television is potentially an excellent source of information, which can be meaningfully incorporated into the school learning process by the effective teacher. It provides a sense of unity for the children who can communicate about the shared experience of watching a particular program. In adolescence the media of radio (for music) and magazines (for styles, and the like) become as important as television. But the effect here, as in adult life, seems to be primarily in terms of how the message is understood, interpreted, and evaluated by the group.

We have seen that much of the influence of mass communication can be understood only by an understanding of the influence of the group on the individual. However, there are other areas where the influence may be more direct. Certainly, the individual's feeling that he is aware of what is happening in the world will have an effect on the way he behaves. Although we do not know specifically how events that occur in one part of the country affect the occurrence of events in other parts, we recognize the role of mass communication in the process. In the summer of 1967, as we elaborated earlier in this chapter, there were riots or civic disruption in almost all the large cities of the United States—many more than had occurred in any year before or after that period. It would be hard to argue that conditions in each of these ghettos reached the point of eruption all in the same summer, or that government policy uniformly brought all these cities to the point of despair. It seems reasonable to suggest that the mass media had something to do with the spreading of the disorder. Watching television reports of riots in other cities, where blacks are seen fighting with policemen and being arrested in large numbers, may have been a factor that added to the frustrations and tensions of the Negroes in cities that erupted before the summer was over.

It is difficult in a discussion such as this not to imply some type of value judgment on the subject matter. We could easily conclude that television is bad because it expands riots, takes children away from their parents, gives young people models of violence, and so forth. Of course, we could come up with a list just as long describing the virtues of the medium. The effects and influence of the mass media are of concern to every generation. The public develops strong feelings about censorship and control of mass communication. Such scientific knowledge as we have about the effects of the media indicates that most of the public attribute much more influence to the media than is actually warranted.[7] For example, in 1970 the Presidential Commission on Pornography[8] reported to the President that their careful investigation into all scientific

---

[7] See the report of the Surgeon General's Scientific Advisory Committee on Television and Social Behavior, *Television and Growing Up: The Impact of Televised Violence*, DHEW Publication No. HSM 72–9090, Washington, D.C., 1972.

[8] *The Report of the Commission on Obscenity and Pornography*, Bantam Books, Inc., New York, 1970.

evidence on the subject led them to the conclusion that pornographic literature has no detrimental effect on those exposed to it, and they recommended against further censorship. President Nixon's response was to refuse to accept the report, and he was quoted as saying that "centuries of civilization and ten minutes of common sense tells me the Commission's report is wrong." In coming to this evaluation, the President was undoubtedly conscious of his many supporters who he felt would never accept the notion that obscene books should not be censored. Thus political considerations may have a more decisive impact on decisions than documented evidence.

SUMMARY

In this book, we have tried to refrain from value statements as much as possible. Rather, we have tried to call attention to what effects seem to result from exposure to the media and to leave it to the reader to determine whether these effects are desirable or not. We have presented some of the ways in which the individual can be influenced as a member of society that do not fit into our conceptualization of the group. The crowd was discussed as having an effect on the individual that can be accounted for by taking into consideration the physical presence of others, the emotional state of an exciting situation or event, and the interstimulation and contagion of such a situation. The individual acts on the basis of aroused impulses, and his actions are aggressive and sometimes destructive.

In contrast, we also discussed mass communication in terms of concern about the influence of an impersonal source of communication upon a dispersed and anonymous audience. We found, in examining the nature of the effect of the mass media, that the persons most influenced by the media are not affected by direct exposure, but rather indirectly, after the message was interpreted by the groups to which the individual belonged. The various media—the radio, television, newspapers, magazines, and books—get a wide exposure in our society, with much of our time being consumed in responding to them. The social psychologist, interested in explaining the effects that society has on the individual, has become aware of the importance of studying mass communication. It is difficult to know just what effects the exposure has on such things as the process of socialization, the operation of the political system, and many other facets of modern life. The knowledge that personal face-to-face influence is almost always more powerful than the influence of the media does not take away from their importance as a secondary source of influence, their potential in other areas such as surveillance of the environment and coordination of the structural components of the society, and their roles in the transmission of the culture.

SUGGESTED REFERENCES

Berelson, Bernard, and Morris Janowitz (eds.): *Reader in Public Opinion and Communication*, 2d ed., The Free Press, New York, 1966.
Series of articles on mass communication and public opinion. Useful reference for professional articles on the topic.

Blumer, Herbert: "Collective Behavior," in J. B. Gittler (ed.), *Review of Sociology: Analysis of a Decade*, John Wiley & Sons, Inc., New York, 1957.
A clear statement of the variety of collective behavior, with a detailed description of the active crowd.

* Headley, Joel T.: *The Great Riots of New York 1712–1873* (1st ed., 1873), The Bobbs-Merrill Co., Inc., Indianapolis, 1970.
Excellent reading. Describes riot behavior in New York more than 100 years ago.

* Katz, Elihu, and Paul F. Lazarsfeld: *Personal Influence*, The Free Press, New York, 1964.
Important research into group influence on the effectiveness of the mass media.

* Kerckoff, Alan C., and Kurt W. Back: *The June Bug*, Appleton-Century-Crofts, New York, 1968.
An excellent descriptive study of the hysterical contagion of a community.

* McLuhan, Marshall, and Quentin Fiore: *The Medium Is the Massage*, Bantam Books, Inc., New York, 1967.
A very popular presentation of the role of the mass media in current society.

* National Advisory Commission on Civil Disorders: *Report* (The Kerner Report), Bantam Books, Inc., New York, 1968.
A readable report on the riots in the United States during the summer of 1967.

Schramm, Wilbur (ed.): *The Process and Effects of Mass Communication*, University of Illinois Press, Urbana, 1955.
Schramm's introduction is one of the most valuable statements of the process of mass communication available.

* Schulz, D. P.: *Panic Behavior: Discussion and Readings*, Random House, Inc., New York, 1964.
The text and readings treat various aspects of panic ranging from psychological factors to disaster research.

* Shibutani, Tamotsu: *Improvised News: A Sociological Study of Rumor*, The Bobbs-Merrill Company, Inc., Indianapolis, 1966.
Investigates the problem of how people make up their minds in ambiguous situations.

* Skolnick, Jerome H.: *The Politics of Protest: A Task Force Report Submitted to the National Commission on the Causes and Prevention of Violence*, Simon & Schuster, Inc., New York, 1969 (paperback: Intext Publishing Group, Ballantine Books, New York).
An important presentation of the history and extent of violence in America today.

Steiner, G.: *The People Look at Television*, Alfred A. Knopf, Inc., New York, 1963.
An interesting research study of the effects of television on opinion and behavior.

* Surgeon General's Scientific Advisory Committee on Television and Social Behavior, *Television and Growing Up: The Impact of Televised Violence*, Department of Health, Education and Welfare, Publication No. HSM 72–9090, Washington, D.C., 1972.
Report of careful research on the impact of television on children. The most thorough analysis to date.

Turner, Ralph, and Lewis Killian: *Collective Behavior*, Prentice-Hall, Inc., Englewood Cliffs, N.J., 1957.
A valuable collection of articles on collective behavior; particularly useful on the topic of crowd behavior.

* Wright, Charles R.: *Mass Communication*, Random House, Inc., New York, 1959.
A short, readable introduction to the study of mass communication.

* References marked with asterisk are available in paperback.

TEN

THE SOCIAL PSYCHOLOGY OF DEVIANCE

A separate chapter devoted to the study of deviance toward the end of a book on social psychology has a number of advantages. It provides an excellent demonstration of how some of the concepts of social psychology can be applied to the understanding of particular social phenomena. At the same time, it gives the reader practice in applying these concepts and, by pointing out some of their subtleties, brings him to a better understanding of the material presented earlier in the book. Finally, it adds a new dimension to our analysis of human social behavior. Even though some forms of deviant behavior can be explained or understood in much the same way as the social psychologist would explain nondeviant behavior, there is usually something about deviance, either as behavior or as reaction to that behavior, that sets it apart from nondeviance.

A basic proposition underlies the social psychological approach to the analysis of deviance: *Nothing about the actions or behaviors in themselves makes them deviant or nondeviant; the judgment placed on an act defines or determines that be-*

havior as deviance. Nothing inherent in any particular kind of behavior establishes the act as deviant; rather, deviance is a property conferred upon the behavior by those who come into contact with it. A person who is not familiar with the culture could identify a particular act as deviant only by becoming aware of the standards of the group or society in which the act is performed. The observation of one man killing another could mean a number of things. The act itself does not determine that the killer is a deviant; the social context does. The killer may be protecting his family, or he may be driving out evil spirits; in some societies, both of these are considered legitimate nondeviant killings. Yet again, he may be killing the man to take his money or as a political assassination; these would be considered deviant in American society.

The study of deviance involves more than an investigation of the individual engaged in a particular act, in the social setting immediately surrounding that act. Just as important is an understanding of the social structure that defines the act as deviant. This approach to deviance, sometimes called *labeling theory*,[1] emphasizes the importance in the labeling process of the labeler as well as the person labeled.

Deviance is a complex phenomenon and cannot be handled thoroughly in one chapter of a short book on social psychology. However, we can suggest how deviance might be understood through the use of social psychological concepts. A number of references are listed at the end of the chapter for readers who wish a more complete understanding.

In emphasizing the social derivation of deviance, we will discuss three types of deviance. First, we will deal with *deviant behavior* that is seen solely as the norm violations of basically nondeviant persons. Second, we will consider the *deviant role*. Here we will be concerned with the situation in which not only is the act considered deviant but also the person who is engaged in the act. He may be seen as playing a role or exhibiting a personality trait; but, as we shall see, the consequence of labeling this person as a deviant is far-reaching. Finally, we will consider the notion of a *deviant subculture,* in which the individual as part of a particular social structure is expected to behave as a member of this subculture in ways that violate the norms of the larger society.

DEVIANT BEHAVIOR AS NORM VIOLATION

In an earlier section on norms and social control, we discussed the methods used by group members to get nonconformists to adhere to the norms of the group. Members of the group use various sanctions that, in one way or another, inform the individual that his behavior is not in line with the expectations of the group and that all would be more comfortable if he conformed to expectations. Here we simply call attention to the fact that responses to deviant behavior can be seen as indicators of the group's definition of certain behavior as deviant; in so doing, group members label that behavior as inappropriate.

We tend to discuss behavior as if it were an all-or-none, either-or phenomenon: either a person has violated a norm or he has not, he is either a conformist or a nonconformist, and so forth. In fact, this level of deviant behavior is not at all simple. First, there is not always consensus in the group as to what is right or what is wrong. Some may feel that certain behavior fits well into the norms of the group, while others may see that same act as questionable, and still others may see it as a clear violation of the norms. Through the process of interaction, which enables group members to see the reactions of others to their acts and the acts of each other, the group may come closer to consensus, but there usually exists some area of doubt.

This is true in part because behavioral norms frequently apply to ranges of behavior rather than to discrete acts. For example, there may be a norm in the college dorms that restricts loud talking after a certain hour. But how loud is loud? Talking between roommates is acceptable. Some arguments may be tolerated, but somewhere there is a line. As long as the behavior is within the tolerance limits, sanctions are not applied, but it is not always easy to determine just where that line should be drawn. It will depend on the labelers, the "others" in the situation; and, to complicate matters more, their responses will vary depending on the situation. A low-status person may feel that the high-status person is acting in violation of the norms but will not say anything; if the dorm supervisor is singing at the top of his voice at two o'clock in the morning, the group may decide that this is appropriate behavior. Often the limits of the norms are not clear until various degrees of deviation occur and we observe at what point negative sanctions are applied by the group.

We could introduce more and more complexities into the analysis of norm violation; however, it seems sufficient that we understand the basic process and that, as we apply this process to actual social situations, we are aware of many subtleties that make the analysis complex but that should not be ignored.

DEVIANCE AS A ROLE

The concept of role is valuable because it is seen as a set of norms that are tied meaningfully together around a position. The concept implies linkages among a variety of acts. It fits these acts together into a meaningful whole and enables us to label the actor as an incumbent in that position. Therefore, the person labeled as a deviant not only will be expected to repeat the deviant act, but in addition can be expected to perform a number of other acts that fit together to make up the role of the deviant. Not only will the person labeled as a drug addict be expected to continue to take drugs, but in addition he will be expected to be careless in his dress, to use a language, or argot, peculiar to drug users, and to find pleasure in activities that are not part of the accepted recreation for "normal" persons.

The labeling process varies in the generalizations that are made about the deviant. Some labelers see the drug addict in terms of a set of specific expectations that not only distinguish him from nondeviants but also distinguish him from other deviants who are not drug addicts. However, this is not always the case. Under some conditions, the labeler will not go beyond using a more general label to indicate deviance. Although he may not use the specific term "deviant," he may have words like "sinner," "no-good," and the like, which he uses to classify—and show his distaste for—a host of diverse but deviant forms of behavior. The person who perceives the deviant in this way is likely to be similarly general about his expectations for the behavior of those he labels as deviant; therefore, he might expect drug addicts to be members of the Communist Party, sexually perverted, and mentally deranged. Such expectations may seem extreme, but they do exist, although most persons in our society are somewhat sophisticated in their responses to deviants. Most persons have a variety of labels for deviant roles that distinguish among a number of forms of deviancy. Regardless of the specificity of the role concept, however, each label links together into a meaningful whole a set of behavioral expectations. In so doing, it "makes sense" out of the behavior of the individual by defining that behavior in a larger context.

Another facet of the role concept follows from this. For every role, particular aspects of behavior, which we can call role *cues*, are keys to role identification. Certain attributes of the actor and features of the situation lead the labeler to define the person as a deviant. The cues need not be the deviant behavior itself; for that matter, they need not be directly related to that behavior. Long hair, using key words, being seen in the presence of particular others may each act as the cues that go into defining the person as deviant. An effeminate gesture may define the homosexual; wearing a knapsack may help to classify a person as a hippie. It is not unusual in our society to use the color of the person's skin as one of the major cues in defining him as deviant.

There are a number of serious consequences of this process of labeling persons as deviant. There are serious violators who are never defined as deviant, while some persons who are labeled as deviant have never engaged in serious norm violation. Studies of white-collar crime have demonstrated that there are persons who clearly and knowingly violate the law as part of their operation of legitimate business. This situation exists at considerable expense to the public; but these persons remain respected members of the community and are never labeled as deviants by their fellow workers, their community, or themselves. On the other hand, there are those who by accident or by factors quite incidental to the person become defined as deviant. The cues used in labeling may have no causal connection to any deviant behavior; a male with long hair who carries a knapsack and talks in "hip" fashion may not use drugs at all, let alone be an addict.

This cannot be taken lightly. One of the most important realizations resulting from this analysis of the labeling process is that the behavior exhibited by those labeled as deviant may be a reflection of the *labeling* itself as much as it reflects actual deviance. Homosexuals band together and form organizations to protect their rights, not because it enhances their sexual enjoyment, but because they have been labeled as undesirables and want to resist the potential consequences. They develop mannerisms and congregate at gay bars, because more open contact would lead to sanctions from those who label them as deviant. Those who lead the fight for the legalization of marijuana make a similar point. They argue that labeling marijuana users as deviant (lawbreakers) defines them in the light of their deviance, thus forcing them to deal with a deviant subculture. This association has far more serious consequence (such as bringing pot smokers into contact with hard drugs) than could possibly be attributed to the physiological effects of the marijuana.

One final consequence of the labeling process should be mentioned. When the person finds himself in a setting in which he is often labeled as a deviant and when his labelers are defined by him as relevant to his life, that person cannot avoid responding to these expectations and adjusting his behavior to cope with the demands that go with his assignment to the deviant role. Therefore, eventually, we would expect the role assignment to have an effect on his self-concept. At some point, he is likely to question his conception of himself; and, if the evaluations of others persist, he may change his self-concept and come to think of himself as a deviant. As we know from Chapter 4, the conception that the person has of himself functions to direct or influence his behavior. When the interaction has moved to the stage at which the individual conceives of himself as a deviant it is no longer necessary for the responses of others to be based on inferences from indirect cues. Now the person will enact the role according to his conception of the expectations for the deviant positions, and others can respond directly to the deviant behavior.

If we consider the various factors mentioned above, we can see that the labeling agent may on occasion be the *determining factor* in some persons' deviancy. To illustrate this, let us consider a hypothetical example showing how the police and the community can become the defining agent in determining the juvenile delinquency of a child. Let us say that two young friends have left their suburban homes and are visiting the city. On their way home they become lost and ask a police officer for help. Since the officer and his assistant are assigned to a district near the boys' homes, they offered to give them a ride in their patrol car. When they arrive, an officer walks one of the boys to the door with the intention of explaining to the parents the circumstances of their presence. However, the parents are not home so the police officers leave without further delay. However, the neighbor across the street happens to be looking out his window when the patrol car stops in front of the boy's house and watches the officer in uniform walk the boy to the door. He had noted earlier that the boy had longer hair than he liked on young men, and he was disturbed about the time the boy had played ball on his lawn. The association with the police officer, the long hair, and the disturbing behavior are the cues that are beginning to lead the neighbor to label the boy as a delinquent. He is adding things up—"making sense" out of his observations. That evening he tells his wife, and they decide not to let their children play with the boy.

So far, nothing of this has come to the attention of the boy himself. As the word spreads, his parents find out that he was brought home in a police car, and they find his explanation somewhat questionable. Later, a child who lives down the street taunts him because his neighbor's children are not permitted to play with him. When his father calls the police to check on his story, he realizes that his parents seriously question his truthfulness and are actually considering the possibility that he is in trouble. Several days later, a boy from down the block (who is known to have a bad reputation both in the community and at school) approaches him and tells him that he knows about his trouble with the police. Although the boy tries to explain, he does not sound convincing; and, before he gets away, the other boy is suggesting that they steal a car for a joyride. He refuses but is struck by the fact that he would be asked to do such a thing. As these types of responses continue, he finds it more and more difficult to respond. Finally, he finds himself lying in an attempt to save face. When he is caught in one of his lies, his parents point out that this confirms their suspicion about the police and other factors that they had noticed. At this point, he begins to seriously question his self-concept. Is he or is he not a delinquent? The final blow comes when the police stop at his house to question him about a burglary in the neighborhood. They had checked with the people across the street and had been told that he had a bad reputation and might well have been the suspect. With this, he is in the beginning stages of conceiving himself as a delinquent. He misses school and sneaks into a movie. Each time he does something of this sort, he confirms for himself the notion that he is a deviant.

Our example is designed to point out how labeling can potentially be self-fulfilling and how the concepts of roles and of self help us to understand the process of deviance.

So far, we have discussed deviant roles as if they were personality characteristics or behavioral patterns that were determined solely by the interactions between the individual and the relevant others. In many situations, the nature of the deviance is related to some characteristic of the individual that is beyond his control. The mentally retarded person and the psychotic are instances of this type of deviance. There is some disagreement as to the origin of such disorders. Some consider the behaviors to be strictly biological in origin while others suggest that they might, at least in part, result from social or psychological deprivation. Regardless of their origin, they are forms of behavior that are not within the control of the individual exhibiting the behavior. In addition, in a society that values intellect and rationality they are seen as undesirable traits and cues of deviance. Again, we must keep in mind that the behavior exhibited by the labeled may reflect the labeling as much as it reflects the actual deviant behavior. With mental retardation and psychosis, the labeling agent may be more formal than in previous examples. The state may declare a person insane, thus telling him (and those about him) that he is deviant. How much of the behavior of a mentally retarded person is due to his lack of intellectual skills and how much is due to the fact that he is labeled by those about him as "deficient" or "feebleminded"?

Physical disabilities as well as psychological disabilities are used as cues for deviancy labeling. The blind, the deaf, and the crippled are all likely to be burdened with deviant labels.

We have pointed out earlier how responses to norm violators are usually directed either at getting that person back into conformity or as a deterrent to others—making it clear that the particular behavior would not be tolerated by the group. Not all deviant behavior evokes this response. In fact, the society sometimes finds it valuable to maintain a number of members classified as deviants. The deviants provide a handy reference point for others' self-evaluation or comparison. Just as useful is their function as scapegoats, to be blamed when things are not going well in society. In our sophisticated society, we do not blame floods and natural disasters on criminals or psychotics, but some do blame the state of the economy on communist agitators and account for their problems in understanding their offspring by suggesting that the children are influenced by sex perverts or drug addicts.

Probably the most common response of those who are labeled deviant is one of disavowal or denial, but this is not always the case. As Ralph Turner[2] points out, under some conditions the deviant role is chosen deliberately, either as a way of coping with a behavior problem or as the lesser of two evils. Alcoholics Anonymous stresses the importance for the alcoholic to admit to himself and to others that he is an alcoholic. This acceptance of the role of deviance gets his drinking problem out into the open where it can be dealt with and controlled.

Another example might be the eccentric person who allows

[2] Ralph H. Turner, "Deviance Avowal as Neutralization of Commitment," *Social Problems,* vol. 19, no. 3, pp. 308–321, Winter 1972.

himself to be regarded as odd, strange, or even "crazy." Although there may be many reasons why persons act in this way, in at least some cases the individual is deliberately choosing the deviant role as preferable to other roles. Perhaps he is afraid that he will be called on to perform in such a way as to reflect his lack of intellectual skills. It may seem more desirable to him to have people see him as "funny" than to take the risk that they might come to see him as "dumb."

Up to this point, we have not mentioned in any detail one type of deviant that is prevalent in our society: the criminal. We will not go into the complexities of the problems of defining a criminal. Here it will suffice to say that we are talking about persons who violate the formal norms (laws) of society. It is interesting to note how the labeling process works for the person who commits a crime, is caught, convicted, sanctioned (serves time), and released. During this time, many labels are applied to him. He is a suspect, a criminal, a prisoner, a convict, an ex-con. All are seen as deviant roles within our society, and all hold their stigma. As with other deviant roles, he may be labeled, according to the specific crime that he commits, as a murderer, a pickpocket, a sex offender, or whatever. When we look into the types of offenses committed by criminals, we find additional variations. For example, the murderer is likely to be an isolated criminal with little or no contact with other criminals. His victim is probably someone he knows, and the statistics show that the odds are he would not commit murder again. In the typical case, the label "murderer" is placed on a person because of a particular act that the person committed sometime in the past. However, the label persists. A murderer is not a person who is likely to go around killing people. He has the label because of what he did in the past. However, the stigma of the deviant label still applies; some will therefore expect him to be dishonest, untrustworthy, and other attributes we link to criminality.

The exception to the case we have described above is the

murderer who is a member of Murder, Inc., or some other element of organized crime, who is hired to murder and engages in this behavior as part of an organized system of relationships. When an individual performs a deviant act as part of any organized role for which that act is prescribed by some subset of the larger society, he is both conforming and nonconforming. In the following section, we will look at this type of deviance.

DEVIANT SUBCULTURES

In a society such as ours, there is likely to be great variation, both in norms and behavior. Occasionally we find within the larger society a subsociety whose norms seem to be patterned to counter the norms of the larger society, if not with deliberate intent at least with little regard for the predominant norm structure. The deviant who is part of a subculture differs from the deviant described in the previous section in that he is conforming to norms that are expected, or even demanded, of him by the other members of his group but that violate the norms of the larger society. The lower-class gang delinquent provides an excellent example of this type of deviance.[3]

There are many varieties of adolescent gangs in American society. We will discuss here some attributes of gangs that seem to be characteristic of urban lower-class boys' gangs. These groups of boys typically hang out on the streets of large cities in America and many other cities of the world. The lower-class neighborhoods in which they are found are characterized by high unemployment, poor schools, and high crime rates. The boys' homes are crowded, and the street seems to be

[3] Albert Cohen, *Delinquent Boys: The Culture of a Gang*, The Free Press, New York, 1955, and David Bordua, "Delinquent Subcultures: Sociological Interpretations of Gang Delinquency," *Annals of the American Academy of Political and Social Science*, vol. 388, pp. 119–136, November 1961.

the most comfortable atmosphere in which they can find companionship. The schools present a particular problem for these boys, because here they are forced to confront the middle-class expectations of the larger society and here they most clearly learn that they will have difficulty competing in the larger society. In many ways, the schools are the epitome of middle-class standards. The teachers are middle-class; the rules are middle-class; and the activities upon which the children are judged as to their worth are especially middle-class—reading, writing, and arithmetic. Modern innovations have, in some situations, helped lower-class children to make up some of their deficiencies in competing on middle-class standards. However, there is little the schools can do about the facts that there are no books in a child's lower-class home, that the vocabulary he hears is limited (at least in terms of middle-class words), and that there is no one pushing him toward career goals (in the professions, for example) that would utilize the things taught in school. So it is here in school that he is made to feel that he has little worth.

In these situations street gangs develop. We do not have space here to discuss much that has been written about these gangs. However, certain characteristics appear in most analyses of gang behavior. Within the gangs certain norms develop that run counter to the norms of the larger society. Particularly widespread are norms that legitimize aggression and encourage offenses against property—stealing and vandalism. Such activities not only are in violation of the norms of the larger society but also appear to be a direct attempt of one segment of the society to act against the dominating majority of that society by collectively deviating from the larger society's norms. In American society, in which material goods and possessions play such an important part in confirming status, stealing can be more than just a way of acquiring needed goods that the gang members could not obtain through legitimate means; it also can be a way for "getting even." Some observers of gang delinquency have suggested that much of the stealing that goes on is *nonutilitarian* in the sense that the material stolen is not something the individual wants or can use, but rather something he steals for the glory and status that his group confers on him for such behavior and, perhaps, for the satisfaction of knowing he is getting back at his oppressor.

The aggressive nature of gang activity can be viewed similarly, particularly actions in response to the demands of the school. In school, quiet intellectual activities are rewarded. On the street, aggressive, fighting behavior is rewarded. The boy who could not compete in the school finds a sense of belonging in the street gang, where there is little ambiguity as to his status and where his skills and abilities are rewarded.

The gang is sometimes referred to as a *counterculture* rather than a subculture, since the behavior of the gang members can better be explained as actions to counter the dominant norms than as a subset of norms within the larger society.

Professional thieves provide a contrasting example.[4] Here we are referring to persons who steal in an organized fashion as their regular business. They may be pickpockets or safecrackers or they may run a confidence game. In contrast to the occasional thief, they are highly trained, they plan carefully, and they succeed by their wit and dexterity. Students of the professional thief have been as impressed with the similarities as with the differences between the thief's behavior and that of the legitimate professional. First, there is a period of socialization during which the potential new thief is tutored by established professionals in the skills and techniques as well as the attitudes and values needed to be a successful professional thief. Once he is accepted by other thieves (as in all professions the acceptance by peers is a necessary condition for

---

[4] Most of this discussion is based on Bill Chambliss, *Box Man: A Professional Thief's Journey*, Harper Torchbooks, New York, 1972, and Edwin H. Sutherland, *The Professional Thief*, The University of Chicago Press, Chicago, 1937.

success), he enters into coordinated activity (professional thieves seldom work alone), in which he not only must demonstrate his wit and dexterity but also must abide by strict standards for behavior and must conform to norms that are unique to his profession. As in all professions, one of the most essential of these norms has to do with mutual protection. The professional thief must always be ready to come to the aid of a fellow professional in need. Of course, the difference between the professional thief and the professional doctor or lawyer is that the activity in which the thief engages to earn his livelihood is in violation of the law.

Deviance, even when highly organized, does not involve total disregard for norms or values. It may take the form of conformity to a highly restrictive set of norms, but these norms are imposed on the individual because he belongs to a particular subsociety that chooses to violate the standards of the larger society. Many of the norms of the deviant subculture are identical with the norms of the larger society or of legitimate subcultures within the larger society. The difference lies in that the deviant group consistently violates some of the key norms of the dominant group. Clearly deviance is not normlessness.

SUMMARY

In this chapter, we considered three types of deviance: simple norm violation, the deviant role, and the deviant subculture. The perceptive reader should be able to apply most of the concepts learned earlier in this book to the understanding of the deviant. Pressures for conformity directed toward the norm violator were discussed in earlier chapters. In this chapter, we emphasized how labeling plays an important part in the establishment and maintenance of deviant roles. This emphasis is consistent with material presented earlier on the importance of language in perception, learning, and role-taking. Similarly, material on the development of the self-concept contributes to our understanding of deviant behavior. The final section of this chapter dealt with subcultural deviance. Here it was pointed out how the group dynamics discussed earlier and some of the processes of socialization apply in the study of the deviant.

SUGGESTED REFERENCES

* Arnold, David O.: *The Sociology of Subcultures*, The Glendessary Press, Berkeley, 1970.
A book of readings particularly valuable for its emphasis on deviant subcultures of various types.

* Baldwin, James: *The Fire Next Time*, Dell Publishing Company, New York, 1962.
Classic statement of the effects of being black in America.

* Becker, Howard S.: *Outsiders*, The Free Press, New York, 1963.
Provides social psychological analysis of deviants with excellent examples of types of deviants and society's effects upon them.

* Cloward, Richard A., and Lloyd E. Ohlin: *Delinquency and Opportunity*, The Free Press, New York, 1960.
One of the first extensive and effective subcultural analyses of delinquency.

Cohen, Albert: *Delinquent Boys: The Culture of a Gang*, The Free Press, New York, 1955.
The first to call attention to the nature of the gang as a reaction of the lower class to the demands of the middle-class society.

* ———: *Deviance and Control*, Prentice-Hall, Inc., Englewood Cliffs, N.J., 1966.
An analysis of deviances with important emphasis on social control.

* Ellison, Ralph: *Invisible Man*, New American Library, Inc., New York, 1952 (Signet Books).
An outstanding novel depicting the consequence of being black in a society that labels black as bad. Also provides an excellent description of the effects of crowd behavior in a riot.

* Goffman, Erving: *Stigma*, Prentice-Hall, Inc., Englewood Cliffs, N.J., 1963 (Spectrum Books).
One of the best descriptions of the phenomenon of labeling and its effect.

* Harrington, Michael: *The Other America*, Penguin Books, Baltimore, 1962.
  The book that led to the poverty program. Can be analyzed in terms of the effects of labeling on keeping persons in poverty.

* Irwin, John: *The Felon*, Prentice-Hall, Inc., Englewood Cliffs, N.J., 1970.
  A symbolic interactionist studies one type of criminal.

* Lemert, Edwin M.: *Human Deviance, Social Problems, and Social Control*, Prentice-Hall, Inc., Englewood Cliffs, N.J., 1967.
  A text covering the concerns of this chapter.

  Polsky, Ned: *Hustlers, Beats and Others*, Doubleday & Company, Inc., Garden City, N.Y., 1967.
  Study of some interesting types of deviants.

* Rubington, Earl, and Martin S. Weinberg: *Deviance: The Interactionist Perspective*, The Macmillan Company, New York, 1968.
  A text and readings. Perhaps the most comprehensive coverage of the social psychological perspective that has been presented in the current chapter.

* Sutherland, Edwin H.: *White Collar Crime*, Holt, Rinehart & Winston, Inc., New York, 1949.
  The well-known criminologist describes the various dimensions of crimes committed by "respected" members of the society.

* ————: *The Professional Thief*, University of Chicago Press, Chicago, 1937.
  An entertaining and insightful story as told by a professional thief with the help of this well-known criminologist.

* Winslow, Robert W.: *The Emergence of Deviant Minorities*, Consensus Publishers, Inc., San Ramon, Calif., 1972.
  Selections from reports of Presidential commissions on crime, campus unrest, causes and prevention of violence, marijuana, homosexuality and prostitution, and obscenity and pornography.

* References marked with asterisk are available in paperback.

ELEVEN

SOCIAL CHANGE

In the preface to this book, I expressed my concern that students see the relevance of the concepts covered and that they be able to apply the principles discussed to their experiences of everyday living. If we are to accomplish this, we must recognize that we are living in the most rapidly changing period in the history of man. Surely this flux in society will have a profound influence on the ways in which society affects the individual and on the influences the individual has on society. Anthropologists tell us man has been in existence for more than 500,000 years. Only in the past 30,-000 years has he created his own tools and lived in structures of his own creation. Only in the past hundred years has he been able to travel faster than a horse runs. Only in the past twenty-five years has he been able to communicate to large portions of the population by way of television and only in the past few years has he been able to travel outside the earth's atmosphere. Whereas it once took several generations to observe significant changes in the structure of society, we now can expect to experience many meaningful changes during our lifetimes.

What effect do these changes have on

our understanding of the social psychological concepts we have discussed in this book? Perhaps this can be best understood by reviewing each section in our text in light of its relevance to social change.

Throughout this book we have claimed that the interaction of the individual with society established and formed the basic behavior patterns that we are concerned with understanding. We pointed out the importance of some understanding of the institutions of society in order to comprehend the effects that society will have on the individual. Now when the dimension of change is added, we can see that this analysis is far more complex than it at first appeared. The analyst has the same problem as a marksman trying to hit a moving target. The institutions that affect the individual's behavior are always changing. Today's families that try to socialize their children as the parents were socialized thirty years ago would run into a continuous series of difficulties.

Depicting the pattern of change in American society as gradually moving from a relatively stable unvarying society to a rapidly altering society may be misleading if we assume that the changes are uniform. To the contrary, what characterizes changes in our society is their discontinuity. Changes in some areas occur much more rapidly than they do in others. Frequently, technological advances have outstripped institutional changes needed to cope with the new inventions. Sociologists describe this condition as cultural lag.

Do these changes in society affect the usefulness of the social psychological principles studied in this text? First, it should be understood that the basic forms and processes of human interaction are not changing. The dynamics of communication, the process of perception, the procedures of role-taking and socialization are the same now as they have always been. However, with the content and structure of society continually changing, these dynamics take on different forms and develop new import as the changes take place. One simple example will suffice at this point. In preindustrial society, parents, in socializing their children, taught them in essentially the same fashion as they had been taught by their parents, and the children learned essentially the same material that their parents had learned. In present industrial society (or in the postindustrial society that is just beginning to emerge), much of the content of what was taught to the parents is no longer relevant for the children. It is not simply a matter of the content of socialization being different from that in preindustrial times; with the rapidity of change, the process takes on new dimensions. Since the present-day parents were socialized into a society that will have profoundly changed by the time their offspring are adults, in contrast to what happened earlier, their roles in the socialization process are diminished and must be shared with the children's peers and such impersonal agents of socialization as the school and television.

SOCIETY

In one of the early chapters, we discussed the relationship between the individual and society. Now we must consider how that society, which is affecting the individual, is changing and how those changes affect the individual. We cannot go into all the dimensions of social change in a complex society. However, we do need to point out some of the more important aspects of present-day society.

It is generally agreed that technological changes that brought on the industrial revolution are primarily responsible for the rapid changes in our lives today. However, we should not conclude that all these changes took the form of material inventions such as the airplane and the computer. Social innovations such as unionism have also played important roles in the changing of society.

Of all the factors that might be mentioned to differentiate technological society from preindustrial society, three seem to be the most significant: *size, heterogeneity,* and *rapidity of changes.* We have tried to emphasize the *rapidity of changes* taking place in modern society. It may well be that by the time this book moves from the author's desk, to the printer, to the distributor, to the bookstore, and finally to you, many changes will have taken place making some of what is said here quite obsolete. The postindustrial revolution, in which man attempts to free himself from the oppression of the machine society, is a popular topic of discussion today. It may be a reality tomorrow.

When we talk of the size of a given society, we are usually referring to all those whose needs are fulfilled through the same network of interrelations. Whereas in preindustrial society the family's needs were almost all taken care of within the family itself, we now are dependent on a complex network that involves most of the world. We rely on food and materials from many countries; we take for granted cooperation in areas of culture, travel, war, and the like. This increase in size of society is made possible by the advancements in technology of many types. With improvements in storage and transportation, it is now possible to have fresh fruit in a restaurant in San Francisco on the same day it was picked in Hawaii. Advances in communication allow us to experience crises "live" on television by way of satellite, when they are happening halfway around the world.

Many of these same changes lead to the *heterogeneity of society.* With increased availability of means of transportation, the individual in modern society is exposed to a much more diverse population than were his preindustrial ancestors. Travel by moderately prosperous Americans has increased tremendously, as have the types of exposures available through the media. Modern man is exposed to a much more heterogeneous population by more than travel and television; the widespread division of labor or differentiation within the society also contributes a great deal to this heterogeneity. It is not so much that a man you meet on the street is likely to be from some foreign, exotic land, as it is that he is likely to be engaged in a specialized occupation or profession that is completely foreign to you. The preindustrial farmer could travel for many miles and encounter many persons without finding anyone who did not live a life very much like his own. In the modern American city, life has become so specialized and compartmentalized that it is not unusual for persons to have little idea what their next-door neighbors do when they go to work. The heterogeneity of society is a reflection of both a diverse social structure and an ever-increasing exposure to a wider range of divergent cultural influences.

So when we are discussing the effect of the society upon the individual it makes a substantial difference whether we are concerning ourselves with preindustrial society or are considering modern technological society. Today that society is large, diverse, and continuously changing.

COMMUNICATION, LANGUAGE, AND PERCEPTION

In the chapter on communication and language, we discussed the importance of a shared set of symbols in order for communication to take place. The latter requires that the words that one person uses must have the same meaning—that is, must stand for the same thing—for him as they do for the person to whom he is speaking. In a large, heterogeneous, changing society, this is no easy task; and misunderstandings are not unusual. In the preindustrial society, objects and experiences did not vary much from one person to another; and, once a set of symbols was learned, it was quite satisfactory for handling most of the encounters in which the individual was required to engage. In modern society, language is continually changing. A few paragraphs earlier we talked about persons being able to watch something "live" on television. Consider the word "live." Only a very few years ago, the word used in that way would not have made sense. Note that in this case a word that had long been a part of the English language was given a new meaning in order to facilitate communication with respect to an innovation within society.

Perhaps what is most significant relative to communication, language, and perception in our modern society is this: In order for modern man to cope with the changing scene—to communicate and to perceive his world—he must continually be expanding his vocabulary. The vocabulary you have obtained at the age of twenty will not be satisfactory when you are forty. Not because you had not had the chance to learn enough words by age twenty, but because in the twenty years between those two ages a large number of new words will be created and many old words will acquire new meanings—not just technical words that might be used in specialized tasks but also words that communicate essential, central concepts that are needed for meaningful dialogue in the society.

It is obvious that keeping up with the new vocabulary is important for communication and perception. However, just as important are knowledge and understanding of the changes themselves and how various groups perceive these changes. It can easily be seen that communication and perception in modern society are much more complex than they once were.

ROLE-TAKING AND SELF-CONCEPTS

Much of what was said about communication also applies to role-taking. In order accurately to take roles, the individual must put himself in the place of the other, take on the other's perspective, and look at himself from that point of view. Remember that the ability to take roles is a function of the individual's familiarity with the other and with the situation in which they are involved. It should be clear from the discussion above that our modern man is faced with many more individuals and situations that are unfamiliar to him. Since this experience starts early in the lives of most of us, it may be that we develop much more refined techniques of role-taking than our forefathers did and thus are better able to cope with modern complexities than would be expected from a simple analysis. We suggested that a diversity of experiences for the child is important in developing his role-taking ability. In role-taking as in communication, the key to coping in modern society is adaptability. Learning new language, new expectations, and new roles is a most consuming aspect of modern life.

We have said earlier that the individual in present-day society can expect to totally change his career several times during his adult years. This is likely to require a considerable change in his conception of himself. No more can he expect to formulate a self-concept that will last him all his life. This change in life organization and self-concept is, of course, more severe for some than it is for others. The business executive who finds at age fifty that there is no longer any use for him in the corporation is likely to find it very difficult to move to a lower-status position, not altogether because he has grown accustomed to the material benefits of the executive position, but also because the power and prestige that were awarded him in his earlier position became part of his image of himself and these self-evaluations will not be given up without pain.

Another dimension of our concern with self-conceptions in modern society needs to be emphasized. In the next section we will bring out the fact that, in our technological society, role differentiation is extreme. This does not simply mean that a person in one role is expected to perform quite differently from a person in another role. What is more important, it also means that a given individual is expected to perform roles that have very little continuity between them. His role as father and husband is completely isolated from his role as salesman, which in turn is independent from his role as a Democrat, and so on. Our preindustrial man could see his life as a single unit. His work, his family, his religion could all be seen as fitting together into a meaningful whole around which he could formulate a consistent conception of himself. In modern society, this is not nearly so simple. His conception of himself most often must be a compromise of inconsistent expectations. It is up to him to put together these variant perceptions that he has of others' attitudes toward him and to develop a conception of himself that will enable him to cope with the requirements of modern living. With the uniform responses of the significant others of the preindustrial man, he had little choice in developing his self-image. Modern man must choose if he is to have a stable conception to live by.

GROUPS

We have said that the primary group with its intimate face-to-face association is important to the individual in a number of ways. His socialization, his conception of himself, and his perspective for looking at the world are all influenced a great deal by this primary group. In present-day society the individual spends a great deal of his time confronted with secondary relations in which the interaction is formal, based on well-defined rules for exchange. This is particularly due to the extreme differentiation of society in which each individual has his own role, which remains somewhat mysterious to the others. When you visit your bank and have an exchange with the bank teller, the complexity of the banking operation makes it close to impossible for you to know what that teller does with his time when he is not confronted with you. Does he read the newspaper until the next customer comes in? Does he run a computer that sorts your checks? Does he go into the vault and play with your money? This is not to suggest that we are completely ignorant of the various operations that go on within society, but rather that there are so many different and complex operations going on that it would be impossible for any one person to know many of them very well. Therefore, it is more difficult for the individual to join in primary relationships with more than a few of those with whom he comes into contact in his everyday life. The family is usually considered the one holdout wherein the primary group remains functional and wherein the individual can be socialized and can develop a conception of himself. However, as we have mentioned earlier, today's individual spends much less time with his family than was true of any previous generation. When you consider the time spent in school, at work, in front of the television set, and with peers, there is very little time left for the family. This is not to suggest that the farm family spent a great deal of leisure time together. The farmer arose at five every morning, and frequently he worked until after dark. If he had had television he would not have had much time for it. By the time his daily chores were done, he was too tired to do much more than go to bed and sleep heavily till the next early morning. However, the work of the farm family frequently included the children. The girl soon took on chores helping her mother; and the boy, when he was old enough, went into the field with his father. Their exchanges were clearly on a primary level and formed the basis for their socialization.

This discussion does not imply that persons do not engage in primary-group relationships in modern society. However, such relationships are likely to last for a shorter duration than was once the case, and the commitment may not be as deep. The commonalities that seem necessary to hold a group together require that these groups be small and homogeneous compared with the rest of society. Because of the broad changes from generation to generation, the family is likely to lose its effectiveness sooner than it once did.

Because of the complexity and diversity of modern society, the individual finds that he must have a variety of reference groups to serve him in forming perspectives to understand his various worlds. His friends at work may form a perfectly good reference group for him when it comes to understanding how to deal with the boss, but they may be of no help whatsoever in learning how to deal with his children. There is some hint that many adults have gained considerable insight to help them cope with the complexities of modern society by using their teen-age children as reference groups by which to perceive the world outside. The young persons who are not burdened with years of preconceived ideas, are in a better position to understand what is going on in modern society than are their elders who are still trying to fit the happenings into their 1950 perspective.

As we said earlier, the individual's roles within society are more precise and more limited than they once were. He is a specialist; however, with the ever-changing technology, he is likely to find his occupational position obsolete and be forced to change his career. Because of the relative isolation of his previous role, this change in status for him is likely to take the form of a personal crisis. However, modern man, compared with his ancestors, is used to changes in his life style, and therefore most people seem to overcome the crises.

With the many well-differentiated roles that the individual is required to enact within society, the likelihood of role-conflict is greatly increased. However, since many of his roles are a result of his interaction with secondary groups in which attachments are for practical rather than emotional commitments, he finds that he can frequently violate expectation with only practical inconvenience but with no emotional conflict.

SOCIALIZATION

We used socialization as an example earlier in this chapter because it seems to bring together the many factors that are relevant to the understanding of the effects of change on the social psychological variables studied in this book. To summarize, we can say that childhood socialization is more complex in a changing society because (1) there is more to be transmitted, (2) the material to be transmitted is not always precise and there is little consensus within society as to its content, (3) the material to be transmitted to the new members of society is not the same material that was transmitted to their parents a generation earlier, and (4) secondary, impersonal agents of socialization play a more important role than ever before.

The one most significant point that we have stressed throughout this chapter is that in a rapidly changing society socialization is a lifetime experience. It does not stop at twenty-one or any other age. Not long ago education throughout life was seen as a luxury that only a very few could be engaged in. Today, some type of education throughout the life span appears to be a necessity. This does not mean that sixty-year-olds need to go back to school; but it does mean that, if that sixty-year-old wants to meaningfully participate in society until he is seventy-five, he will have to learn the meanings of many new words, adapt to new means of transportation, and tolerate new forms of behavior that he cannot conceive of now.

Social change frequently finds one institution lagging behind others in adaptation to changes. Right now, science and technology seem to be far ahead of the social institutions. Religion seems to be struggling for its survival. The economic and political institutions frequently appear to be failing us by their inability to cope with the realities of our changing societies. Perhaps socialization institutions—the family and education—will prove to be the most flexible and will lead the way to a meaningful adjustment to our present condition. Regardless of what the future holds, those persons who comprehend the dynamics of interpersonal relationships—the subject matter of this book—will best be able to cope with the changing society.

NAME INDEX

SUBJECT INDEX

Abstractions, 59–60
Adolescence, 170–173
Aggregates, 98–99
American Journal of Sociology, 31
American Sociological Review, 31
Anthropology, 7–8
Aroused impulses in crowds, 187
Awareness, 113

Balance theory, 111
Biological influences in socialization, 152
Biological potential, 48–49
Bureaucracy, 115–117

Categories, 98–99, 142–143
Categorization in perception, 61–62
Children:
  raised in isolation, 153
  role-taking ability of, 78
Classification, linguistic, 62
Cohesiveness, 138–140, 145
Collective behavior, 181–192

Communication, 53–56, 77, 193, 229–230
  definition of, 53
  and perception, 65–67
  of social psychological findings, 30–33
Conditioning in early childhood, 157
Conformity, 130, 135
Consciousness, 163
Consensus, 55–56, 207
Contagion in crowds, 187
Content analysis, 28–29
Counterculture, 218
Crowds, 181–192
  acting, 183–192
  casual, 183
  conventional, 183
Cultural determinism, 38, 40
Cultural lag, 226
Culture, 11, 45, 57

Deviance, 205–222
Deviant behavior, 206
Deviant role, 206, 208–216
Deviant subculture, 207, 216–219